C|

of
FIRE

Books by Clarence E. Macartney

Chariots of Fire
Great Women of the Bible
The Greatest Texts of the Bible
He Chose Twelve
Paul the Man
Strange Texts but Grand Truths
12 Great Questions About Christ

CLARENCE E. MACARTNEY

CHARIOTS *of* FIRE

kregel
PUBLICATIONS

Grand Rapids, MI 49501

Chariots of Fire by Clarence E. Macartney.

Published in 1994 by Kregel Publications, a division of Kregel, Inc., P.O. Box 2607, Grand Rapids, MI 49501. Kregel Publications provides trusted, biblical publications for Christian growth and service. Your comments and suggestions are valued.

Cover and book design: Alan G. Hartman

Library of Congress Cataloging-in-Publication Data
Macartney, Clarence Edward Noble, 1879–1957
   Chariots of fire / Clarence E. Macartney.
     p.   cm.
   Originally published: 1951.
   1. Bible—Biography—Sermons. 2. Sermons, American.
3. Presbyterian Church—Sermons. I. Title.
BS571.5.M33   1994   252'.051—dc20   94–12728
                                              CIP

ISBN 0-8254-3274-x (paperback)

1 2 3 4 5 Printing / Year 98 97 96 95 94

Printed in the United States of America

CONTENTS

FOREWORD

In previous studies in the field of Bible biography, I have taken up practically every major character in the Bible. This book, therefore, deals with Bible men and women who, while not the preeminent characters of the Bible, either for good or for evil, are full of interest.

It has been my experience that when it comes to preaching, many of the lesser-known personalities of the Bible draw the preacher's bow for him with greater power and more striking illustration than the more familiar and more celebrated personalities. When, for example, the theme is retribution, who better than Adoni-Bezek, who mutilated his prisoners by cutting off their great toes and in turn had his great toes cut off, can teach the lesson of retributive justice? Or if the theme is motherhood, who better than Rizpah can touch our hearts with a mother's devotion as we see her keeping watch over the bodies of her two sons who had been hung by the Gibeonites, suffering neither the birds of the air to rest on them by day nor the beasts of the field by night? Or if the theme is secret sorrow, who better than Jehoram, who had sack-cloth within, can tell us of such sorrow? Or if the subject is slander, who more than Doeg the Edomite has the poison of asps under his tongue? Or if the subject is God's sleepless providence, who better than Hagar in the wilderness can tell us that God's eye is upon us?

CLARENCE E. MACARTNEY

1

CHARIOTS OF FIRE— ELISHA'S SERVANT

"And Elisha prayed, and said, Lord, I pray thee, open his eyes, that he may see. And the Lord opened the eyes of the young man; and he saw." (2 Kings 6:17)

When the young man looked the first time, all that he saw was horses of flesh and blood and chariots of iron. But when he looked the second time, what he saw was horses and chariots of fire. The same young man, the same eyes; but now his eyes had been opened.

A true man of God is worth more to a nation than a battleship, a regiment of soldiers, or a squadron of bombers. This truth is illustrated in the history of the prophet Elisha, the first man to whom was given that great title, the "man of God."

Ben-hadad, king of Syria, the inveterate and congenital enemy of Israel, had invaded the country on several occasions. But every time he was about ready to pounce down upon the king of Israel and capture his army, the king of Israel received warning and withdrew his army to a safe fortress. This happened so many times that Ben-hadad came to the conclusion that there was a traitor in his camp. He summoned his officers and captains, and demanded of them to know which of them was for the king of Israel. One of his officers said to him, "None, my lord, O king: but Elisha, the prophet that is in Israel, telleth the king of Israel the words that thou speakest in thy bedchamber."

When Ben-hadad learned this, he saw that the real enemy whom he must capture first of all was not the king of Israel, but the prophet Elisha. One of his spies informed him that Elisha was staying in the town of Dothan. Benhadad immediately put his army on the march for Dothan. All through the night the army marched, and the chariots rolled toward that stronghold. Before the sun had risen, Dothan was completely surrounded by the Syrian army.

Early in the morning the servant of Elisha, probably a student in the school of the prophets taught by Elisha, went up on the wall of the stronghold to take a look. What he saw there filled him with terror. Wherever he looked—east, west, north, south—the Syrian army was encamped. Dothan was surrounded by a cordon of iron. The light of the sun, just rising over the eastern mountains, was reflected from the dashboards of the chariots and the shields and helmets of the soldiers. The young man could hear the rumbling of the chariots, the neighing of the war horses, and the shouting of the officers. In great alarm he ran down from the wall to the house where Elisha was staying and told him what he had seen. "Alas, my master! how shall we do?"

Elisha answered calmly, "Fear not: for they that be with us are more than they that be with them."

The young man must have looked at Elisha with astonishment. Perhaps he wondered if his master was losing his mind. "Just we two against the whole Syrian army! And yet Elisha says that they who are with us are more than they who are with them!"

Then Elisha made his prayer to God. "Lord, I pray thee, open his eyes, that he may see." And the Lord opened the eyes of the young man, and he saw; and, behold, the mountain was full of horses and chariots of fire round about Elisha. The Syrian army, in answer to the prayer of Elisha, was smitten with blindness. Elisha led them in helplessness to Samaria, the capital of the nation, where their eyes were opened again. There they were dismissed and sent home in humiliation to their own country.

This page from the biography of Elisha is a striking demonstration of the reality and power of spiritual forces. We have no need to be taught the reality and power of material forces. The newspapers, the magazines, and the events of the day are constantly advertising, praising, and exploiting the power of material forces.

But these are not the only forces; for, though real, they are visible, and therefore temporal, for "the things which are seen are temporal." The real powers are the invisible powers. The real forces at work in the world are spiritual and moral forces. Our great need as a nation, as a Church, and as individuals is to have our eyes opened to the presence and reality and might of spiritual forces.

THE NATION'S SPIRITUAL FORCES

Going up on the wall and rampart of our nation's life we behold in whatever direction we look a Syrian army, as it were, threatening the nation's life. This nation has stood in the past upon moral and spiritual foundations. But if these foundations are destroyed, what shall the nation do? How fares it today with these foundations?

In America today a major crime is committed every twenty-two seconds, a murder every forty minutes. Revelations in our great cities tell of a formidable and vast underworld of organized crime, and even of criminals who share their ill-gotten gains with officers of the law—appointed to protect society from their depredations. Everywhere this terrible cancer is preying on the body of the republic. How long can the nation stand it? When we hear of these conditions, we recall what Lord Macaulay wrote to a friend in New England. Rome was destroyed by Goths and Vandals from without, he said, but America's Goths and Vandals would come from within.

We are faced, too, by the breakdown of the home. One in every four marriages ends in divorce. The ancient curse of strong drink finds more victims than ever before, and casts its blight today over hundreds of thousands of women as well as men. We think, too, of the flood of licentious literature which is pouring over the nation. Fifteen thousand sex magazines are now published every week in this country! We have, too, in our midst those who owe an allegiance to a higher authority than our own government, and who have a vast enthusiasm for the "No God."

When we think of all this, we feel like crying out, "Alas, my master! how shall we do?" Yet the nation goes on; it still stands; it still carries the hopes of millions here and millions in the other parts of the world. God must be with America. He must have a purpose

for it today and tomorrow, as he has had in the past. At the end of
the Civil War, Secretary of War Stanton caused an illumination to
be displayed from the dome of the unfinished Capitol, with the
words of Psalm 118, "This is the Lord's doing; it is marvelous in
our eyes." We take hope and courage because we believe that back
of all material power and resources are the resources of God. Our
hope is not in parties or legislatures but in the recognition of, and in
obedience to, the spiritual and moral laws which have exalted this
nation and made it great. In a western city where a great meeting
was to be held in a public auditorium to set forth the purpose and
plans of the Crusade for Freedom, a member of the city council
raised an objection because a minister of the gospel had been invited to take part in the program. He did not think that religion had
anything to do with the Crusade for Freedom. A Crusade for Freedom in America without religion, without the fear of God, will be
only a mockery, a tinkling cymbal and a sounding brass. "Not by
might, nor by power, but by my spirit, saith the Lord." "Except the
Lord build the house, they labor in vain that build it: except the
Lord keep the city, the watchman waketh but in vain." Lord, open
the eyes of our people, open the eyes of our governors and senators
and legislators, that they may see and may own those spiritual forces
which are our hope and salvation.

In another crisis in the history of Israel centuries later, when
another army, the army of Sennacherib, had invaded the land, the
godly King Hezekiah strengthened the defenses of the city and
spoke these words of encouragement to his captains and leaders:
"Be strong and courageous, be not afraid nor dismayed for the
king of Assyria, nor for all the multitude that is with him: for there
be more with us than with him: with him is an arm of flesh; but
with us is the Lord our God to help us, and to fight our battles."
When the people heard these words, they "rested themselves upon
the words of Hezekiah." So must it be with us today. We must
"rest ourselves" on our faith in moral and spiritual powers and in
God's plan for the nation.

THE CHURCH AND SPIRITUAL FORCES

When we climb up on the bulwarks and the towers of the
church and look abroad, in every direction we see hostile forces

drawn up against the church: the discounting of the moral law and the unseen world; the relaxing of the moral authority of the Bible; unbelief in cardinal facts of the Christian revelation; an invasion of ritualism and formalism and an exaltation of the symbols of the Christian faith, which in a strange way accompanies the disregard of the doctrines of the Christian faith which those symbols declare; the passing of the Lord's Day; the passing of religion and prayer from the home; and a vast indifference and disloyalty on the part of the membership of the churches. Everywhere there is a falling away from the plain preaching of sin, judgment, redemption, and eternal life. Hence there are many who are wondering about the future. "Watchman, what of the night?" How can we withstand this ever-rising tide of worldliness and paganism? "Alas, my master! how shall we do?" How long can the church stand?

The answer is, just as long as we can see that the horses and chariots of fire are on our side; just as long as God cares for his church; just as long as we have the seven thousand who have not bowed the knee to Baal. As for a church which conforms itself unto this present world, which preaches another gospel which is not another—it little matters what happens to that church. But as for the church which is the "church of the living God, the pillar and ground of the truth," and which declares the glorious mystery of godliness—"God was manifest in the flesh, justified in the Spirit, seen of angels, preached unto the Gentiles, believed on in the world, received up into glory"; the church which proclaims Jesus Christ the same yesterday, today, and forever, supernaturally conceived and brought into this world, his divine rank and mission certified by great signs and wonders, who offered himself through the eternal Spirit upon the cross as a sacrifice for our sins, who rose again from the dead the third day in the same body in which he suffered, and showed himself alive to his disciples by many infallible signs; who ascended into heaven and sitteth on the right hand of God the Father Almighty, where he ever liveth to make intercession for us; the church of the Savior, who shall come again in great glory with his angels and in the clouds to overthrow every stronghold of Satan and to restore all things, when the whole earth shall he filled with the knowledge of the glory of the Lord as the waters cover the sea—as for that church we have no fear. The stars in their courses are fighting for her. As God said of the church through his prophet Isaiah, "No weapon that is formed against thee shall prosper."

> Though earthquake shocks are threatening her,
> And tempests are abroad;
> Unshaken as eternal hills,
> Immovable she stands,
> A mountain that shall fill the earth,
> A house not made with hands.[1]

OUR PERSONAL LIFE AND SPIRITUAL POWERS

How many foes there are which threaten and assail our own lives, even as the Syrians that morning surrounded and threatened Dothan of old! How many temptations there are, how many pitfalls and snares of Satan, how many thorns in the flesh or spirit, how many waves of adversity and sorrow, and how many clouds of doubt come floating by, obscuring the heavens. "Without fightings, within fears." "Alas, my master! how shall we do?"

How shall we do? We shall do through Christ, of whom it was said, "Greater is he that is in you, than he that is in the world." We shall do through him who inspired that apostle who leaned on his breast at the Supper to say, "This is the victory that overcometh the world, even our faith." We shall do through him who, when awakened by his frightened disciples that night on stormy Galilee, arose in majesty and, speaking first to the elements, rebuked the winds, and they folded their wings, and said to the waves, "Be still," and they fell flat on their faces. Then turning to his disciples he said, "Why are ye so fearful? how is it that ye have no faith?"

This young man, the servant of Elisha, who was frightened when he saw the Syrian army, was probably a student in the school of the prophets. He could have passed a fair examination in theism and theology. But it was only when his eyes were opened, only when he saw the invisible, that he was able to pass an examination in practical theology and so take hope and courage. When his eyes were opened by the prayer of Elisha, he saw all that Elisha saw. This is an inspiring thought for you and me. You may not have the personality or ability of an Elisha, an Elijah, a Peter, a

---

1. A. Cleveland Coxe.

John the Baptist, or a Paul; and yet if your eyes are opened, you can have their faith, and you can see all that they saw.

If God be for you, who can be against you? God keeps faith with trusting souls. When they were burning Protestants in England during the persecutions of Bloody Mary, a young lad was being burned one day at Smithfield. In his distress he called out to a bystander, "O sir, pray for me!"

The cruel man answered, "I would as soon pray for a dog as for a heretic!"

"Then," said the suffering youth as he lifted his eyes heavenward, "O Son of Man, wilt thou shine upon me!" And at that moment, through the clouds of the dark and overcast day, the sun in the heavens shone forth. A beautiful picture, a symbol as it were, of how "light is sown for the righteous, and gladness for the upright in heart." Trust in God, who says to you in the midst of your trials and troubles, "Cast thy burden upon the Lord, and he shall sustain thee." Trust in Christ, who said to Paul when he besought him to pluck the thorn out of his flesh, "My grace is sufficient for thee."

A great scene in Bunyan's immortal allegory of the soul's pilgrimage and warfare tells how Christian and Hopeful, weary with the rough way they were traveling, left it and went over to Bypath meadow, where it was easy to their feet. But when the night came on, they found that they were lost. Falling asleep under a tree, they were seized by Giant Despair and thrust into the dungeon of Doubting Castle. After several days' imprisonment, and as they continued in prayer, Christian suddenly broke out and said to his companion, "What a fool . . . am I, thus to lie in a stinking dungeon, when I may as well walk at liberty! I have a key in my bosom, called Promise, that will, I am persuaded, open any lock in Doubting Castle." Then Christian pulled it out of his bosom, thrust it in the lock, and opened the door. And so they came again to the King's highway.

How often we are like Hopeful and Christian in that dungeon, when all the time we have in our bosom the key called Promise, which can open the door and set us at liberty. Lord, open our eyes that we may see the reality and power of spiritual forces. Lord, open our eyes that we may see that we are compassed about by a cloud of witnesses who in thy name have come off victorious.

Lord, open our eyes that we may see beyond the horizon of this world that "better country, that is, an heavenly," where is our inheritance, incorruptible, undefiled, that fadeth not away. Lord, increase our faith! Lord, open our eyes that we may know the power of prayer!

> But there's a power which man can wield
> When mortal aid is vain,
>
> That power is prayer, which soars on high,
> Through Jesus, to the throne,
> And moves the hand which moves the world,
> To bring salvation down.[2]

---

2. John Aikman Wallace.

2

A TROPHY FROM MARS HILL—DAMARIS

"A woman named Damaris." (Acts 17:34)

Among the celebrated paintings of Raphael is one of Paul preaching at Athens. The apostle is seen standing on marble steps facing the temple of Mars, before which is the statue of the god of war. Paul is shown here not as a man of mean personal presence, as his enemies at Corinth had intimated, but as a man of commanding appearance. Both hands are uplifted as he addresses the philosophers on the great theme of Jesus and the Resurrection.

Just in front of Paul stands one of the Epicureans, listening with rather a friendly countenance, and a not hostile curiosity. His head is turned slightly to one side. Next to the Epicurean stands a Cynic, leaning on his crutch, his head resting on his hands on top of the crutch, and in his face malignant anger and disgust. To the right of him is a Stoic, his arms folded under his mantle and his splendid head bowed down. His eyes are closed, and he is absorbed in reflection.

Back of the Epicurean are two young men, one with a look of supercilious scorn on his face, the other with a look of disgust. To the right of the Epicurean is a man whose head is bowed down. His countenance has the appearance of one who is impressed with Paul's truth and eloquence, but his pride prevents him from confessing it. The forefinger of his right hand is pressed against the upper lip, as if to impose silence upon himself.

Immediately to the left of Paul is a young man with outstretched hands pointing toward the apostle and engaged in heated discussion with those around him. Back of Paul are three figures, one a corpulent man wearing a cap, his face heavy and sensual. In the midst of this group of three is a magician, and kneeling at his right is a man with a wicked, malignant countenance whose expression would indicate danger for the apostle.

At the extreme right, and at the other end of the circle, are the two who believed, and who cleaved to Paul, Dionysius the Areopagite and "a woman named Damaris." Dionysius, kneeling with uplifted hands and face, is the incarnation of devotion, enthusiasm, and affection for the apostle. At the right is Damaris, a woman with luxuriant hair, full bust, and fair countenance, looking with modest devotion upon the apostle whose doctrine she has received.

Ever since Luke in this chapter in the Acts described for us Paul preaching on Mars Hill, men have wondered about those two persons, the only fruits of Paul's preaching on that memorable occasion, especially the woman named Damaris. Imagination strives to sketch her person, her spirit, and her subsequent history, but this is all that we know about her. She appears for a moment on the stirring stage of the apostle's life and then vanishes. We never hear of her again. Yet of all the noted scholars and philosophers who listened to Paul on that occasion, save for that other believer, Dionysius, she is the only one whose name has survived.

Paul's pastorates were of necessity very brief. On this his first invasion of the continent of Europe he was driven out of Philippi to Thessalonica, and out of Thessalonica to Berea, and out of Berea to Athens. The sun of Athens' dominion and splendor had set long before this visit of Paul. Corinth was now the chief Greek city, and Rome was the center of the world's power. But Athens was still the center of the world's culture. Paul did not plan to remain long in Athens. Silas and Timothy, who had come with him to Athens, had gone back to Macedonia, and Paul was waiting at Athens to learn from them if he could return to Macedonia. But while he was waiting, he walked about over the city and was stirred and shocked to see it given over wholly to idolatry. He must have seen plenty of idols at Antioch and Philippi and Thessalonica, but never such a multitude of them as he saw now at Athens. It was a popular saying that it was easier to find an idol in Athens than it was to find a man. First of all he went into the synagogue and talked and disputed with the Jews, but not about idols, for they would all agree with him on that point. But in the market places, where the philosophers were wont to talk and discuss the problems of the universe, he met some of the Epicureans and the Stoics and talked with them. Some looked upon him as just a joke, a freak, a babbler, and said to one another, "What will this babbler [word pecker] say?" They likened him to a sparrow or a rook hopping about from place to place pecking seeds from the rocks. To others it seemed he had a new god to import and add to the pantheon of the gods, already so liberally furnished at Athens. He talked so much about "Jesus, and the Resurrection" that they concluded that perhaps both Jesus and the Resurrection were new gods. For this reason they invited him to set forth his views on Mars Hill, at the Areopagus. Before a new god could be worshipped and proclaimed, the court of Areopagus had to pass on its claims. Either Paul was asked merely to tell about his new god to the judges of the court, or he was actually on trial before them as a setter forth of new gods.

Mars Hill is a considerable elevation to the west of the Acropolis. Standing on this hill Paul commanded one of the great panoramas of the world. Behind him, to his left, was the almost perfect Doric temple of the Theseum, still preserved. Directly across from him to the east was the Acropolis, with the noble Propylaea for a gateway, and crowning the hill the Parthenon, the temple of the virgin goddess Athena, and alongside the Parthenon the great image of Athena, holding the mighty spear which had been made from the trophies taken from the Persians at the Battle of Marathon five hundred years before. Below, to the left of the Acropolis, was the rock-hewn theater of Dionysius where the Greek tragedies were acted. To the northeast were the mountains which looked on Marathon; and toward the south the port of Athens, the Piraeus, and the Island of Salamis. In those waters the Greek navy sank the ships of Xerxes as he sat, a melancholy spectator, on his mountain seat. Such was the pulpit from which Paul delivered his memorable sermon.

He found his text on his way to the meeting. It was an inscription on one of the innumerable idols, "To the Unknown God." When Paul read that, he said to himself, "How true that is, and how sad, too." This gave him his start. To a people who had hundreds upon hundreds of idols for gods, and yet knew not God, because the world by wisdom can never know God, Paul determined to proclaim the true God.

GOD THE CREATOR

Telling them how he had seen this inscription on one of their altars, and how he had noted that they were a very religious people, he said, "Him declare I unto you." He preached to them first of all God as the creator and upholder of the universe. The philosophers were accustomed to talk with one another about emanations and rotations and aeons and atoms. But here Paul proclaims to them the truth of God as the Creator of the universe. He commenced where the Bible commences, "In the beginning God." The world is not eternal. It had a beginning, and God was the beginner and the Creator. He is the Lord of heaven and earth, and made the world and all things that are therein. There Paul stated the first truth of our Christian creed, the sublime affirmation of the Apostles' Creed, "I believe in God the Father Almighty, Maker of heaven and earth."

From that he proceeded to say that the Lord of heaven and earth did not dwell in temples made with men's hands, even so beautiful a temple as that which they had reared, or their fathers, to their supposed goddess, Athena. Neither could he be worshipped with men's hands, as though the Lord of heaven and earth, who gives to all life and breath and all things, had need of anything that man could give him. To understand the boldness of that utterance, we must remember where it was delivered—not in Pittsburgh, Chicago, London, but in the very heart of Athens, and within a stone's throw of its most sacred shrine and temple, and where all about him were the shrines and idols and altars and temples which had been embellished with the genius of Phidias, Praxiteles, and Apelles. It was there, in the very midst of these idols, that the heroic apostle declared the folly of idols. Paul once spoke of himself as "entrusted with the gospel," and never did he more magnificently justify that trust than that day when he stood on Mars Hill and, pointing off towards the Parthenon and the great image of Athena, and with the statue of Mars within a few feet of him, declared that the attempt to reach God through these things was vanity.

From that he proceeded to declare God's providence. Since God created the world and the human race, the human race is one. The Jews divided mankind into Jews and Gentiles; the Greeks into Greeks and barbarians; the Romans into Roman citizens and the rest of mankind. But here Paul declared that God hath made of one blood all nations, and that the differences between nations and races are as nothing compared with their identities.

This led him on to say that God is not only the Creator of the universe, but its upholder and governor. History is not an accident. God had determined beforehand the times before appointed and the bounds of their habitation, that they should seek after God. Greece was not an accident, any more than Jerusalem, or Rome. The great movements of history are not without the permission of God, nor do they fail to register his will. The drama of time is God's drama, and the great men, the great nations, the great movements, and the crises of history are but the brief embodiment or the transient realization of his will.

These great utterances were introductory to the main part of Paul's sermon, which was repentance before God and faith in Jesus Christ. God, he said, is not far away, dwelling like Jupiter in the clouds on Olympus, but is near to us by his Spirit, "not far from every one of us." Men ignorantly had thought of the godhead as gold or silver, or stones graven by man's art and man's device. But now God calls upon all men everywhere to repent of their sins. There is a day of judgment coming, and in that day, when God puts a stop to human history, Jews and Greeks and barbarians and Romans, princes and philosophers and peasants, must all appear. God "hath appointed a day in which he will judge the world in righteousness, by that man whom he hath ordained." The proof of this was the resurrection of Christ. That was the great witness "whereof he hath given assurance unto all men, in that he hath raised him from the dead."

That was enough for the philosophers. They had heard Paul with some patience and courtesy up to that point, as long as he spoke on the general themes of creation and providence and the unity of the human race. But when he became personal, and in the name of God called upon them to repent, and gave as the proof of his message the fact that God hath raised Christ from the dead, they would hear him no longer and broke up the meeting. Paul left their proud assembly and went down the stone steps of the Areopagus perhaps somewhat sad at heart, yet with the satisfaction of knowing that he had not shunned to declare unto them the whole counsel of God.

His sermon had produced different reactions among his hearers. Some of them mocked; others of them said, "We will hear thee again of this matter." But there were two who believed and cleaved unto him. These three attitudes—derision, delay, and decision—represent the different receptions which the hearts of men give to the gospel. Give Paul credit for this at least: his preaching was so clear and definite and unmistakable that there was something in it that men could mock at, if they wanted to, and something, too, that called for a decision; and that is more than can be said for some messages which are proclaimed today.

DERISION

Take first the attitude of derision. These men who mocked at him were, in the professional sense, interested in abstract truth and science and knowledge in general. But when they heard a man in dead earnest like Paul call upon them to repent, and tell them that they must all appear in judgment before Christ, they laughed at him. About all you can do for a mocker is to pray for him. The first psalm says that the man is blessed who sitteth not in the seat of the scornful. Jesus was mocked in his day. When he told them that he was going to raise the daughter of Jairus, they "laughed him to scorn." Yet we remember that although the two thieves both mocked at him on the cross, there was one of those thieves whose heart the Holy Spirit touched, and it was he who prayed, "Jesus, Lord, remember me when thou comest into thy kingdom," and it was to him Jesus said, "Today shalt thou be with me in paradise."

DELAY

The second attitude was that of delay. There were those of Paul's auditors who did not abruptly and completely dismiss him and his message, but said, "We will hear thee again of this matter." The New Testament places a rather low estimate on those who are interested enough in religion and the gospel to think about it, but who fail to make a decision, "ever learning, and never able to come to the knowledge of the truth." On another memorable, and much later, occasion Paul preached to the Roman Governor Felix and his paramour, Drusilla, and preached such a sermon on righteousness and temperance and judgment that Felix trembled. But instead of coming to a decision and repenting, and believing on God and Christ to eternal life, he too said he would hear Paul again on that great matter: "Go thy way for this time; when I have a convenient season, I will call for thee."

When the great truths of Christianity are presented to us, it is always dangerous to do what those philosophers did when they said, "We will hear thee again of this matter." In the first place, you may never again hear anyone present the gospel to you. Some of those philosophers were never able to climb Mars Hill again, perhaps, or feel the fresh wind from the sea upon their faces. Who knows? And if they did, they never heard Paul preach again. He passed on from Athens to Corinth, and while we know that he once passed through Athens at a later date, there is no record of his ever having preached again in that city.

In the second place, it is dangerous to say, "We will hear thee again of this matter," because, even if you do hear again, the disposition of your heart may be different. The soul, like the soil, has its favorable seasons, and for the gospel of eternal life that favorable season is always today. Felix, we know, did hear Paul again. He kept him in prison for two years and communed often with him. But never again did Paul make Felix tremble. All that Felix was interested in now was getting a bribe out of some of Paul's friends. That was his tragedy! Once not far from the kingdom of heaven under the mighty preaching of Paul, but now his only interest in the preacher was to use him to get money out of his friends!

Dr. William Paxton, on a summer stay at Bedford Springs, Pennsylvania, had long conversations with the then president of the United States, James Buchanan, on the subject of Christianity and the claims of the gospel. At the end of these conversations the president said that his conviction was that Christianity was true, and that when he finished his term of office he proposed to make a confession of his faith. "But, Mr. President," Dr. Paxton said earnestly, "the gospel says 'today' not 'tomorrow.' Now is the accepted time."

DECISION

The great majority of Paul's hearers either mocked or derided, or delayed and postponed. But there were two who believed and cleaved unto him: Dionysius, a member of the court which met on Mars Hill, and "a woman, named Damaris." Why did these two believe while all the others mocked or postponed? Who can answer that question? Jesus said, "The wind bloweth where it listeth, and, thou hearest the sound thereof, but canst not tell whence,, it cometh, and whither it goeth: so is every one that is born of the Spirit." The only answer that we can give is that the wind of the Spirit was blowing that day over the rocky summit of Mars Hill and used the preaching of Paul to sow the seeds of repentance and eternal life in the souls of Dionysius and Damaris.

We wonder about that woman named Damaris. Was she the wife or the daughter of one of those philosophers who heard Paul that day? How did she happen to be there? Was it possible that she was one of those gifted, intellectual women, neither wife nor slave, but companion to philosophers and learned men, and who could discuss with them the mysteries of the universe? We get the impression that she had a mind naturally inclined to high things. Perhaps she had been baffled with life's perplexities and disappointments. Perhaps her companions or lovers had failed her and disappointed her. But now she has found the true companion and the eternal lover. Did she ever see Paul again? Is she perhaps one of those women of whom Paul speaks, who labored with him in the gospel and whose names are in the book of life? Of that last, at most, we can be certain. She cleaved unto Jesus and her name is written, never to be blotted out, in the Lamb's book of life.

It took courage and self-denial for her to come out on the side of Christ and of Paul. It meant that she no longer had the fellowship of the intellectual aristocrats and philosophers of Athens, but had now for her associates and companions slaves and artisans, poor and humble folk. Yet in their fellowship she found a happiness and a joy which she had not found in the company of the philosophers, because in this company of the "not many wise men after the flesh, not many mighty, not many noble," she had the fellowship and the friendship of Christ.

If we knew the subsequent history of Damaris, it would tell us of the great issues and influences which can come from the life of a talented and attractive and strong-minded woman who gives her heart to the Lord. How much the church of Christ owes to women like that! And how much it needs such women today! Never was there an age when the cause of Christ needed more the influence and the labors of women who choose him rather than this passing world with its glittering but soon-fading show and splendor. Such a woman was the daughter of a governor of Delaware, a woman of high intelligence and station. Her great beauty was the occasion of a tragedy among her admirers, resulting in the death of one of them. No woman was more regular or faithful at all the services of the church than she—not just formal Sunday morning services, but Sunday night and prayer meeting and all the set and appointed services of the church. Once I remarked to her that it was an encouraging thing to see a woman who could move in altogether different circles and give her time and interests to other interests and institutions, so faithful and devoted to the church. What she said by way of reply was, "I have been all through the other. I know all about it. There is nothing in it."

No! The great realities are those of the Christian life, and in the Christian associations. The woman called Damaris chose Christ, and because she did, her name is spoken of nineteen centuries later. She is the subject of a sermon and the occasion of an appeal to other women to follow in her footsteps and give up the world for Christ and cleave to him. Is there a woman today who is ready to do that? Can any of those Stoics or Epicureans be named who invited Paul to preach to them that day on Mars Hill? Not one of them! But the name of Paul still lives, and the name of Damaris, who chose Christ and eternal life, still lives, and will live forever, because her name is written in the Lamb's Book of Life.

3

THE RESURRECTION OF CONSCIENCE—HEROD ANTIPAS

"John, whom I beheaded: he is risen from the dead." (Mark 6:16)

Men do not rise from the dead until the Resurrection. But Herod Antipas, the ruler of Galilee, was convinced that John the Baptist had risen.

This is the reason why he was sure that John had risen. Herod Antipas and some of his friends and nobles were reclining on couches on the balcony of Herod's palace at Tiberias. An occasional slave came in, bringing them wine to drink. In front of them stretched the blue Sea of Galilee, and far in the distance rose the brown mountains of Gadara. As they sat looking out over the sea, they engaged in desultory gossip: the winner of the last chariot races at Antioch; the bread riots at Alexandria; the latest news from Augustus in Rome; guesses as to why the stepson of Augustus, Tiberius, was studying rhetoric at the Island of Rhodes; what Archelaus, the older brother of Herod Antipas, and king of Judea, was doing, or plotting.

Then, suddenly, the conversation shifted to another personality. One of these nobles, Josephus, said, "Have you heard the rumors about Jesus, the Nazarene?"

Olynthus, leaning against the balcony rail, answered "Yes, I hear strange, incredible tales about him—cleansing lepers, healing lame men, opening the eyes of the blind."

26

Marcellus, who was reclining next to Herod, asked, "What do you make of it all?"

Whereupon Josephus said, "Some think that he is Elijah. The book of Malachi predicts, you know, that Elijah will return."

"And others," added Olynthus, "think that he must be Jeremiah. There was a tradition, you know, that Jeremiah would appear with a golden sword and put it into the hands of a leader of the Jews."

"And still others," said Marcellus, "think that he must be the prophet Samuel; and still others that he is Nathan."

While this conversation was going on, Herod, with a troubled look on his face, had risen from his couch and was pacing up and down behind his friends, between their couches and the palace wall. At length he turned and, confronting them, said, "You are all mistaken. He is not Elijah, nor Jeremiah, nor Samuel, nor any of the other prophets. I will tell you who he is: John, whom I beheaded: he is risen from the dead! This is John the Baptist come out of his grave!"

Why did Herod think and fear that Jesus was the resurrected and risen person of John the Baptist? This is the reason why: Herod had taken his brother Philip's wife and was living with her in sin. John heard of it and with splendid courage strode one day into the palace and, confronting the king, and in the presence of Herodias, said to Herod, "It is not lawful for you to have your brother's wife. You are breaking the commandment of God, and God will punish you."

This startled Herod. Herodias wanted John killed at once, but Herod shrank from doing that, for his conscience told him that what John had said was true. Instead of killing John, he shut him up in the prison. Frequently too, and probably when Herodias was absent from the palace, Herod had John brought up out of his prison, and asked him to preach to him. What a strange preaching that was! The lonely and austere prophet and forerunner of Jesus reasoned with Herod of righteousness and temperance and judgment to come, just as Paul did when he preached to Felix and made him tremble. The record is that Herod feared John, "knowing that he was a just man and an holy, and observed him; and when he heard him, he did many things, and heard him gladly." We take it from that that the preaching of John had a wholesome effect upon Herod, and that he refrained from doing certain evil things because of the influence of John upon his soul.

Unfortunately, however, there came a day, Herod's birthday, when he had a great party to which he had invited his "lords, high captains, and chief estates of Galilee." It was a royal feast indeed, and it had royal entertainment with it: acrobats, clowns, jugglers, dancers, and singers. But the most thrilling feature of the feast Herod had reserved for the last. The curtains at one end of the palace opened, and out stepped the beautiful Salome, the daughter of Herodias. She came before the king's seat at the banqueting table, bowed before him and then, arrayed in her filmy robe, began the dance, whirling about, faster, and faster. At length the dance came to a climax as Salome wheeled in front of Herod and flung her bejeweled arms into the air. The palace rang with the approving shouts of the lords and nobles as they pounded on the table in their delight. When the applause had subsided a little, Herod leaned over toward Salome and said, "Salome, that was wonderful! The best I have ever seen! Ask what thou wilt, and I will give it to you, even to the half of my kingdom!"

When Salome had gone out, one of the lords sitting next to Herod, heated with wine, said to the king, "Herod, wasn't that promise a little dangerous? It might cost you more than you think."

Herod replied, "Oh, well; what of that! The girl will ask for a cashmere shawl or some gold of Ophir earrings; perhaps a black slave from Numidia; a chariot; or something of that sort. What if she does? The dance was worth it, wasn't it?"

"Yes," said the half-drunken lord, "it was worth it, and I would give the half of my estate to see it again!"

Clapping her hands, and with her body still vibrating from the movements of the dance and her eyes aflame with excitement, Salome said to Herodias, "Mother, I have just finished my dance before Herod and his lords. When I was through, he said that he would give me anything I asked for, even to the half of his kingdom! What do you think of that! Mother, what shall I ask?"

"Ask the head of John the Baptist!"

The light of expectation faded from the face of Salome as she said, "No, not that, Mother. That would not please me. I wanted—"

"No matter what you want, Salome. It is not what you want, but what I want; and what I want is the head of John the Baptist!"

The hum of conversation ceased when the curtains parted again and Salome came in and took her stand before the king. Everyone was eager and curious to know what she was going to ask. Bending toward her, Herod said, "Well, Salome, what is it? What are you going to ask?"

"The head of John the Baptist! Give me the head of John the Baptist in a charger!"

When Herod heard that, his face, inflamed with the wine, blanched, and the goblet shook in his hand. "No; not that, girl. Not the head of John, that righteous man! Ask anything else, or the head of anyone else; but not the head of John, that man of God!"

But when Herod said that, the nobles and lords began to remind him of his promise. One of them said, "Don't be a welsher, Herod! Don't go back on your word. Remember that you promised to give the girl anything that she asked."

Now comes one of those great sentences which only the Bible can utter. It is this: "And the king was sorry." The king was exceedingly sorry. The king within man's breast, his conscience, his better self, is always sorry, and always mourns when we are about to yield to temptation. That is the deepest sorrow of all, the sorrow of the king within us! The knowledge of good, the reverence for good, mourns over the evil within us.

The king was exceedingly sorrowful. Yet for his oath's sake, and for their sakes which sat with him, and for the sake of Herodias, Herod gave his consent. Summoning an officer of the guard, he said to him, his voice sounding as if it came out of the tomb, "Go! Bring the head of John the Baptist in a charger!"

Down in his dungeon the lonely John heard the tread of the officer and the two soldiers coming down the winding stone steps to his cell. Then he heard the sound of the iron key as it was thrust into the door. John thought to himself, "Herod is sending for me again to preach another sermon to him. What shall I choose for my text this time?"

Yes, John, you are going to preach another sermon to Herod; but this will be thy last and thy greatest sermon, a sermon the accents of which will echo forever and ever.

And there it is! The head of John the Baptist in a charger, as Salome holds the silver charger up before the, king with that ghastly trophy upon it. Don't turn away, Herod! Here it is! This is what you asked for! Don't avert your eyes! Look, Herod! Here is the head of John the Baptist! Forever thou wilt see this head; in the midst of thy pleasures and dissipations, in the discharge of your duties as the tetrarch of Galilee; at brightest noonday, and in the watches of the night. Look, Herod! This is what thou shalt see!

That was why it was that when Herod heard of the mighty works of Jesus and caught some echoes of what Jesus said to the people, he was frightened, and his conscience smote him. Brushing aside the theories and explanations of his lords and nobles, and the opinions of the people that Jesus must be Elijah, Jeremiah, or some other of the great prophets come back to life, he exclaimed, "John, whom I beheaded: he is risen from the dead!"

That was a mighty tribute to Jesus, that Herod should have identified him with John the Baptist, whom Jesus declared the greatest man that ever lived. It was also a high tribute to John. But more than that it was a magnificent tribute to the power of conscience in the soul of man. Jesus was not John, and John had not risen out of his grave; but conscience convicted Herod and made him think that John, whom he had murdered, had come to life again.

There are those who try to tell us today that conscience is just a leftover, or remnant, of man's animal history. According to this theory, when one member of the herd, or group, chose to go its own way, a different way from the herd, he had a fear of incurring the wrath of the others. So conscience arose. I wonder if the men who with elaborate terminology invented such a theory of the origin of conscience, themselves felt the pangs of conscience for such a denial of the truth? A single pang of conscience, a single incident like that of Herod Antipas, thinking when he heard of the preaching of Jesus that John had risen from the dead, is sufficient to dismiss such a definition.

> Yet still there whispers the small voice within,
> Heard through Gain's silence, and o'er Glory's din:
> Whatever creed be taught or land be trod,
> Man's conscience is the oracle of God.[1]

---

1. Byron, "The Island."

There is a beautiful verse in the Proverbs which says, "The spirit of man is the candle of the Lord." Another, and perhaps a better translation is, "Man's conscience is the lamp of the Eternal." In the conclusion to his *Critique of Pure Reason*, Immanuel Kant wrote, "Two things fill the mind with ever new and increasing wonder and awe—the starry heavens above me and the moral law within me."

THE ROLE OF CONSCIENCE

In the story of the first temptation the moment the tempter suggested to the woman that she take and eat of the forbidden fruit, and that, instead of dying, her eyes would be opened, conscience flashed its warning light, and the woman immediately responded that God had said they could eat of all the trees in the garden except the tree which was in the midst of the garden, and that if they did eat of it they would die. The woman was not left in doubt as to the right or wrong of the suggestion of the tempter.

Conscience uttered its faithful and warning voice when Joseph was confronted by that fearful temptation in the house of Potiphar, and when all temporal and earthly considerations—such as promotion to honor in Egypt, the absence from his own people and their way of life, the natural inclinations of the flesh, and the fear of vengeance if he refused—were on the side of yielding. Yet Joseph obeyed the voice of conscience and uttered his memorable defiance to temptation which still rings through the ages, "How can I do this great wickedness, and sin against God?"

Conscience uttered its voice and its warning when Pilate ascended his judgment seat and was confronted in the early light of that memorable Friday morning by Jesus. Conscience at once said to Pilate, "This is an innocent man." His private examination of Jesus confirmed that verdict, and its was further strengthened by the message which Pilate got from his wife as he resumed his place on the judgment seat, "Have thou nothing to do against that just man: for I have suffered many things this day in a dream because of him."

The real tragedies of life are primarily due to the disregard and rejection of the warnings of conscience. There are those who have always held to a belief in the doctrine that each soul has its guardian angel. But, however that may be as to the angels, it is true that every man has a guardian angel in his conscience. Oh, how much of the misery of mankind would be lifted and banished, and how much greater and deeper would be the cup of man's joy, if he obeyed his conscience! Robinson Crusoe was not only a great storyteller, but a great teacher of religion. He speaks of "secret hints and pressings of mind" which came to him to direct him in the way he should go, when his own sense, his own inclination, and his apparent temporal interest called him to go the other way. "I afterward made it a certain rule with me that whenever I found those secret hints or pressings of mind, I never failed to obey the secret dictate, though I knew no other reason for it than that such a pressure, or such a hint, hung upon my mind."

> What Conscience dictates to be done,
> Or warns me not to do;
> This teach me more than Hell to shun,
> That more than Heav'n pursue.[2]

THE JUDGMENT AND PUNISHMENT OF CONSCIENCE

Conscience instructs and guides and warns; but when its voice is rejected, then conscience becomes a judge. Conscience pursues; conscience smites; conscience punishes. Conscience, which a moment ago was your best friend, now has become your worst and implacable enemy.

When Andrew Jackson was preparing for his duel with Dickinson, whom he killed in the duel, a friend sought to dissuade him from fighting the duel, reminding him that he had heard that Aaron Burr never had peace of mind after he had killed Alexander Hamilton on the "tragic shores" of Weehawken.

The punishments of conscience consist of the withering up and clouding of any joy a man may take in what he has kept or has gained by the violation of conscience. Another punishment of conscience is fear. We see that at the very beginning. It was sin, disobedience to conscience, which gave birth to fear. When the man and the woman had broken the commandment of God, and

---

2. Pope, "Universal Prayer."

"heard the voice of the Lord God walking in the garden in the cool of the day, [they] hid themselves from the presence of the Lord God amongst the trees of the garden." Is this an ancient myth? Or is it as modern as the fear and remorse of the last transgressor of this day?

When conscience is dismissed and rejected as a guide and a friend, it comes back in the form of remorse. When the man and the woman were driven out of the garden, a flaming sword which turned every way flashed and flamed at the gate of the garden. Alas, how many have vainly tried after their transgression to get past that flaming and flashing sword of conscience which keeps the way of the Tree of Life! How many times I have heard on the lips of others the poignant and despairing cry of remorse. Poe's raven that came out of the darkness and perched upon a bust of Pallas, just above his chamber door, and whose only word was, "Nevermore," appears to be a symbol of remorse. He beseeches the raven,

> Take thy beak from out my heart, and take thy form from off my door
> But all that the raven answers is, "Nevermore."
> And the lamplight o'er him streaming throws his shadow on the floor;
> And my soul from out that shadow that lies floating on the floor,
> Shall be lifted—nevermore.

Judas knew the punishment of conscience. Conscience had warned him against his fearful crime; and when he had committed that crime, the thirty pieces of silver burned his hand and burned his soul; and he flung them down in despair before the priests and scribes, exclaiming as he did so, "I have sinned in that I have betrayed innocent blood!"

THE REWARDS OF CONSCIENCE

There is no reward comparable to the reward of conscience. There is no earthly decoration comparable to the "well done" of your own conscience. But the rewards of conscience are not won without paying a price. When, in Victor Hugo's great tale, Jean Valjean after an all-night battle with conscience went to the court where an innocent man was about to be sentenced to prison, and

Jean Valjean confessed that he himself was the guilty man, some thought he was mad; others pitied him for the sacrifice he was making. But he turned to the courtroom and said, "You all, all who are here, think me worthy of pity, do you not? When I think of what I have been on the point of doing, I think myself worthy of envy. God, who is on high, looks down on what I am doing at this moment, and that suffices."

Joseph obeyed conscience and had to pay the price. The price was an infamous accusation by a wicked woman, and after that the dark and stinking dungeon of Pharaoh. But then comes the great sentence, "But the Lord was with Joseph." God was with Joseph in the prison! That is the great thing—to be where God can be with you, whether it be a prison or a palace. And soon Joseph was out of the dungeon, and Pharaoh's gold chain was about his neck. Those angels are still at work forging that golden chain for all who obey conscience and are faithful to God. Jesus knew temptation, knew it in behalf of all men; and when he had resisted the tempter and was true to God his Father, "then," as Matthew puts it in that sublime conclusion to his account of the temptation, "the devil leaveth him, and, behold, angels came and ministered unto him."

In view of all this, how important it is to make friends with conscience, for a friendly conscience is a mighty aid in the battles and trials of life. Paul said, in two memorable utterances, that he had "lived in all good conscience before God." And again, "Herein do I exercise myself to have always a conscience void of offence toward God and toward men." That means that he strove, struggled, agonized, so that he might have a conscience void of offense toward God. In one of his last messages he returned to this subject of conscience, and warned Timothy, and men today, to hold to "faith, and a good conscience, which some having put away concerning faith have made shipwreck." How hard do we struggle and strive to have a conscience void of offense toward God and man? We pray for faith, for courage, for perseverance, for other virtues of the Christian life; but do we ever pray for that great blessing of God, a good conscience? When God speaks through conscience, we should obey his voice. So the psalmist said he tried to do: "When thou saidst, Seek ye my face: my heart said unto thee, Thy face, Lord, will I seek."

4

SLEEPING IN CHURCH—EUTYCHUS

"And there sat in a window a certain young man named Eutychus, being fallen into a deep sleep." (Acts 20:9)

Sound asleep! Fallen into a deep sleep, and under such a preacher as Paul!

The passage which records the slumber of this young man is the most illuminating record in the New Testament of early Christian worship. From it we learn that the disciples, even at this early date, had begun to celebrate the resurrection of Jesus by meeting together on the first day of the week. At this service, or assembly, they broke bread together, celebrated the Communion, and listened to a sermon.

Paul was on his way to Jerusalem, on his return from his third missionary journey, which had taken him as far as Greece. He had crossed over from Macedonia to Troas, and there remained long enough to meet with the Christian disciples in that city and celebrate the Communion with them. We can be sure that the presence of Paul brought out to that evening service everyone in Troas who was able to be there. Imagination likes to dwell upon the scene. Since Paul in his last letter from Rome asked Timothy when he came to stop at Troas and get the old robe that he had forgotten and left behind him at the home of Carpus, we can be fairly certain that it was in this home of Carpus that the meeting was held. It must have been a house of considerable dimensions, as it had three stories. We can see the eager congregation assembled in that large upper chamber, with a window open toward the moonlit Aegean. Then there were no grand organs, no altars, no choirs, no stained glass; just the plain assembly of the people, and the truth of God. Many of them were, no doubt, slaves, and all of them probably had toiled at their daily labor on that Lord's Day.

In the room many lamps, virgins' lamps, are burning, not only to give light, but to protect the Christians against the popular slander that they met in the darkness to celebrate their feasts to the accompaniment of licentious and immoral conduct. The central figure, of course, is Paul. Some of those who are present we know—the friends who are accompanying him to Jerusalem. These are Sopater from Berea; Aristarchus and Secundus from the church at Thessalonica; Gaius and Timothy of Derbe; Tychicus and Trophimus from Asia, probably Ephesus; and Luke, who tells the story. A table is in the foreground, spread with the bread and the wine. The light of the swinging lamp falls on the face of Paul and shows the marks of the suffering and hardship he has endured since first he came to Troas when he had his dream of the man from Macedonia and crossed the sea to find him.

We have no record of Paul's sermon on this occasion, but we can be sure that, as everywhere, he preached Christ and him crucified, exhorting the disciples to love one another, to be godly in their daily living, and to look for the coming of the kingdom of God.

The clock had not yet been put on religious services as it is today. People went then to a Christian assembly just as they go today to social meetings, or popular entertainments, with no thought of how long it was going to last, but expecting to remain unto the end. That night Paul preached a long sermon. Luke says he "continued his speech until midnight." Perched high up at the window was a young lad named Eutychus. Boylike, he had taken this conspicuous but dangerous seat, where he could see and hear everything. But as Paul was long preaching, and the hour was late, the room close, and the atmosphere stifling with so many lamps burning, nature asserted itself. The young man became drowsy and at length fell into a deep sleep. In his sleep some fancy or dream must have come to him; and, starting up suddenly, he lost his balance, grasped vainly at the window sill, and with a cry plunged headlong from the window. The congregation gave a horrified ejaculation. Then in a moment there was the ghastly thud of the body striking the pavement three stories below. At once the congregation broke up, and Paul and everyone else hurried down the winding stone stairs, their lamps and torches held high in their hands, to render what aid they could, and above the shuffling of the feet and the murmuring of the crowd were heard the loud cries of the boy's father and mother.

Paul, who was always a man for the emergency and who could do other things than preach, when he arrived on the scene where the boy had been taken up for dead, told the crowd to stand back and give him air; and then, like Elisha, he embraced the lad, saying that his life was still in him. This was soon apparent, and in a little while the boy was himself again, no worse for his fall of three stories. When he had restored the boy, Paul led the crowd back up the stairs to the upper chamber and resumed his interrupted sermon. After this they celebrated the Communion, and Paul again preached to them until the break of day, or, as Homer would have put it, Homer who sang of great events at this same Troy ages before, "the rosy-fingered dawn" came up over the sea.

This is the first record we have of a man who slept in church. He has had a multitude of successors; but this is the first recorded instance of one who fell asleep under a sermon. And if a preacher should sometimes behold a sleeper in his congregation and be inclined to blame himself, it will be some consolation to him to remember that even great Paul cast a man, and not an old man, but a youth, into so deep a sleep that he fell three stories to the ground, and but for the miracle of Paul would have perished. However, concerning those who sleep in church, there are not only those who sleep physically in church, but those in the church and around the church who are asleep under its great voice and its great opportunity. They sleep under the preaching of the gospel; their bodies wake, but their souls sleep.

MEN WHO ARE ASLEEP TO THE GREAT OPPORTUNITIES OF THE CHURCH

All about us in the churches are those who are asleep as to their opportunities for Christian service and the performance of Christian duty. Once a man and his wife wrote their pastor to express their satisfaction in the services of the church, but said that they were merely spectators. Merely spectators! And how many of them there are. These persons not only fail to perform their duty, but miss the joy of working for Christ in his church. A sleeping soldier at the battle front may be armed with the latest weapons; but if he is asleep, he is good for absolutely nothing to the army and to the cause. Christ asked Peter and James and John to watch with him in his agony. But they fell into a deep sleep and heard not his cries of woe and his pathetic prayers, and thrice Christ had to arouse them out of their slumber. And when he awakened them the third time, their opportunity for serving him in that particular capacity was gone forever. So far as that was concerned, Christ could then say to them, "Sleep on now, and take your rest."

Again, there are those who are asleep as to the opportunities for friendship and the joys of the associations of God's house. Those who are awake to this know that in church are formed the most delightful and most abiding associations. The highest friendships are formed where those who delight in one another's fellowship also delight in the Lord and love the Lord.

> Blest be the tie that binds
> Our hearts in Christian love.

MEN WHO ARE ASLEEP TO SINFUL HABITS AND EVIL LIFE

This is something that, however strange it may seem, often exists. There are men who hear the gospel, its sharp division between good and evil, its warning against sin, its call to repentance, and yet at the same time are under the spell and infatuation of evil. An evil habit may be fastening its coils about them, and they are unaware of it, unaware at least of the danger and the death in it. Every now and then you hear of some Christian whose character has broken down, who has fallen into transgression; and yet that man was often in church. He listened with apparent interest to the sermon and in his heart did not reject the truth. How can you account, then, for this breakdown and this fall? The only explanation is that he was morally and spiritually asleep. Jonah slept in comfort in the hold of that pitching vessel on the way to Tarshish, while all the seasoned seamen on the deck above him, fearing that they were going to perish, called upon whatever gods they knew to save them out of their distress.

Burglars when they rob a house sometimes chloroform those who dwell there so that they may rob and loot at their pleasure. It would seem that Satan acts in much the same way when he despoils men of their souls. He casts them into a deep sleep, gives them a false sense of safety, the conviction that while temptation and evil might destroy others, it could never destroy them. It is while men sleep that the Devil does his work. It was when Sisera, exhausted after the great battle of Kishon, lay asleep in the house of Jael where he had taken refuge, that that patriotic Hebrew woman took a hammer and drove a tent pin through the temple of the captain of Canaan. It was when Samson lay asleep on the lap of Delilah that the Philistines sheared him of his locks and stripped him of his great strength, and put out his eyes and cast him into the dungeon to do the work of a slave. "Yet a little sleep, a little slumber, a little folding of the hands to sleep: so shall thy poverty come as one that travelleth and thy want as an armed man." Satan has no worries about a Christian who is asleep. In a dream once a man saw a church with one devil asleep in the cupola of it. Then he came to a humble cabin that was surrounded by a company of evil spirits. When he asked the explanation, he was told that one devil was sufficient to look after a sleeping church, but that it required a great company of evil spirits to watch against that humble cabin where one man was on his knees in prayer.

Satan would rather cast a man into a deep sleep than destroy him in any other way, because in this way there is no resistance on the part of the victim. Recall the disastrous retreat of Napoleon from Moscow in 1812. The best account we have of that retreat is by Armand Caulaincourt, the Duke of Vicenza, who was Napoleon's Master of Horse, and was with him in intimate contact all through the Russian campaign. Caulaincourt describes how the soldiers of the Guard, overcome by the cold, fell out of the ranks and lay prostrate in the snow, too weak or too numb to stand. Once they fell asleep, they were dead. To sleep was to die. He relates how on a number of occasions he tried to arouse men who had thus fallen to the ground, warning them that they would perish; but the drowsiness engendered by the cold was irresistibly strong. To all his entreaties the drowsy soldiers were deaf. The only words they uttered were to beg of him for the love of God to go away and let them sleep. So is it with the sleep of the soul, with the fatal allurement of temptation and of sin.

MEN WHO ARE ASLEEP TO GOD AND TO ETERNAL LIFE

It is quite possible to listen to the pronouncement of the tremendous truths of the gospel, calling for repentance and faith and obedience, pointing out the gulf that is fixed between men in the next world, and yet both the will and conscience be sound asleep. The preacher becomes unto men as Ezekiel said, a "lovely song," and they are as deaf to the warnings of the gospel as the adder is to the music of her charmer. They hear, having ears; and yet in a sense, hear not. There is no resolution, no determination, no repentance. When the sermon in church is over, life follows up that sermon with its own great and eloquent sermons. Those sermons that are constantly sounding in men's ears—sickness, peril, affliction, providence, death—all say to the soul, "Hear what the preacher says." But the sermon of life produces no more effect on them than the sermon in church. If Luke were to describe some of our congregations today, he would have to tell of not one but many who have sunk down into a sleep far more perilous than that into which Eutychus fell. Hence it is that we hear the cry of the gospel to awaken out of sleep. Go from the church asking yourself, not, Did my friend or neighbor in the church hear that? or, If he heard it, was he asleep under it? but, Am I asleep? In Christ's last sermon he told of those virgins who slept away their chance to meet the bridegroom and be admitted to the supper. It is easy to sleep away your chance of eternal life. You need not go out and commit some great crime. You need not consult the works of atheists and infidels and adopt their principles and unbeliefs. All that is necessary to lose eternal life is to sleep.

Luther had a parable or dream of how on one occasion the Devil sat upon his throne listening to the reports of his agents and ambassadors and what progress they had made in opposing the truth of Christ and destroying the souls of men. One spirit said there was a company of Christians crossing the desert. "I loosed the lions upon them, and soon the sands of the desert were strewn with their mangled corpses."

"What of that?" answered Satan. "The lions destroyed their bodies, but their souls were saved. It is their souls that I am after."

Then another made his report. He said: "There was a company of Christian pilgrims sailing through the sea on a vessel. I sent a great wind against the ship which drove the ship on the rocks, and every Christian aboard the ship was drowned."

"What of that?" said Satan. "Their bodies were drowned in the sea, but their souls were saved. It is their souls that I am after."

Then a third came forward to give his report, and he said: "For ten years I have been trying to cast a Christian into a deep sleep, and at last I have succeeded." And with that the corridors of hell rang with shouts of malignant triumph.

If anyone is asleep—asleep as to his high and beautiful opportunities in the church of Christ, asleep as to some evil habit that ere long will strangle him with its coils, asleep as to eternal life and eternal salvation—then let him hear these words of God, "It is high time to awake out of sleep. . . . Let us therefore cast off the works of darkness, and let us put on the armour of light." "Awake to righteousness, and sin not." "Awake, thou that sleepest, and arise from the dead, and Christ shall give thee light."

5

GOD'S COMPENSATIONS— AMAZIAH

*"But what shall we do for the hundred talents which
I have given to the army of Israel?"* (2 Chronicles 25:9)

Amaziah, the king of Judah, was getting ready for war. Will the day ever come when nations will cease to get ready for war? Certainly not until the day comes when they will begin to get ready for peace. Peace must be prepared for just as much as war. But this time—and, alas, all through the ages—it was a case of getting ready for war.

The young King Amaziah stood upon a platform in front of his palace as his army passed by in review. It was a mighty host, 300,000 of them. Their helmets, breast-plates, swords, and lances flashed in the brilliant sunlight. Company after company, regiment after regiment, marched past the royal reviewing stand, their banners waving in the morning breeze. It was a brave spectacle, and the people cheered their king and cheered their soldiers. Amaziah was about to invade and chastise Edom, the hereditary and congenital enemy of Israel. But 300,000 men did not seem to him a large enough army. To augment the ranks of his army he hired 100,000 more soldiers, most of them men of Ephraim, from the kingdom of Israel, at that time given over to idolatry and apostasy, and under the disfavor of God. But that apparently made no difference with Amaziah. As long as these 100,000 soldiers could fight, it made no difference to him where they came from or what their relation was to the God of Israel.

Then appeared upon the scene a man of God. Nothing could be more stirring and dramatic than the appearances which the man of God makes in the history of the Old Testament. Sometimes he is named, as in the case of Elijah or Elisha. More often he is unnamed. All that we know of him is that title, a "man of God." He appeared to Eli, the aged priest, and pronounced judgment upon his house because of his wicked sons. He appeared to Ahab, who had let Ben-hadad go, and in the guise of a wounded soldier pronounced the judgment of God upon him. He appeared suddenly at the golden calf of Jeroboam at Beth-el and pronounced God's judgment upon that altar of idolatry, and doom upon those who niinistered there.

Here the man of God appeared to Amaziah and remonstrated with him for employing soldiers from apostate Israel. The man of God owes nothing to the world. He fears nothing from the world. He speaks as the representative of conscience. He cannot be frightened. He cannot be cajoled or bribed. His judgments are inescapable You have all heard the voice of the man of God speaking through conscience, the "still small voice" in your breast.

When the man of God warned Amaziah that his war would end in defeat and disaster if he employed these soldiers from Israel, and advised him to dismiss them and send them back to their own country, Amaziah said, "But what shall we do for the hundred talents which I have given to the army of Israel?" Immediately the man of God answered, and there must have been a touch of irony in his answer, "The Lord is able to give thee much more than this."

Reluctantly, sorry to get nothing out of his one hundred talents, Amaziah sent the 100,000 men back to their own country. In the expedition against Edom which followed he was completely successful; but his victory was marred by an act of great brutality when he hurled 10,000 prisoners to their death over a precipice.

The victory which Amaziah had won turned his head. When he got back to his own country, he brought with him the gods of the Edomites, and, setting them up in Jerusalem, bowed himself down before them and burned incense unto them. Then another man of God appeared. Oh, these men of God! If we could only get rid of them! If we could only do evil, and nothing be said about it! If conscience could give its approval! Or if we could only get rid of conscience, how much unrest and unhappiness we could escape! But you cannot get rid of conscience. You cannot keep the man of God from your door. Now he came and asked Amaziah why he had made such a fool of himself as to set up and worship these gods of Edom which had not been able to deliver their own people out of his hand. The foolish king angrily dismissed the man of God and told him to mind his own business. He then proceeded to challenge to battle the powerful king of Israel, Joash, saying, "Come, let us see one another in the face!" In the battle which ensued Judah was overwhelmed, the capital was sacked, and Amaziah was brought in disgrace a prisoner into Jerusalem.

A DUAL PERSONALITY

Amaziah affords one of the most striking studies in double personality. Those master biographers of the books of Kings and Chronicles always commence their biographies of the kings of Israel and Judah by a summary and definition of their character. In all other biographies the method is the reverse. In secular biographies and histories the story of the man's life and achievements is told, and then at the end is the summary as to his character. But these Old Testament biographies begin the other way. They commence by saying that this or that king did that which was right, or that which was evil, in the sight of the Lord. They want us to know at once what the man's real character was, and what was the drift of his life. Sometimes the verdict, "And he did that which was right," or "did that which was evil in the sight of the Lord," is amended, and the man is presented as not wholly committed to good or evil. This was true of King Amaziah. The chronicler says of him, "He did that which was right in the sight of the Lord, but not with a perfect heart." That does not mean that the chronicler is telling us that Amaziah was not a perfect man. For that matter, who is? What he means to tell us is that although Amaziah had regard for the word of the Lord and, as in this instance of the army of Israel, obeyed the word of the Lord, he had strong inclinations the other way. When he did obey the word of the Lord, it was with reluctance, with a strong desire that it had not been necessary. This prepares us for what followed: his complete and open defiance of the word of the Lord as spoken to him through the prophet.

But let us not throw stones at Amaziah. There is much of Amaziah in all of us. We would not totally disregard God and the commandments of God, but can we say that our hearts are wholly set to do his will? Do we not sometimes wish that we could be rid of these moral and spiritual laws? Yes, there is something of Amaziah in all of us.

What interests us today, particularly in the history of Amaziah, is that incident about the one hundred talents. When the man of God told him to dismiss the army that he had hired with those talents, and warned him that defeat would follow if he did not do so, Amaziah obeyed the command and heeded the warning; but he did it very unwillingly. "What shall I do," he said, "for the one hundred talents with which I hired them?" One hundred talents is a big sum of money. Just to send this army home will be throwing good money away. What shall we do for the one hundred talents? How is that loss going to be made good?

Here, again, Amaziah is a very modern character. He was thinking first of consequences, instead of thinking first of principles. He was thinking of worldly and temporal loss, instead of obedience to the will of God. This is a very common thing.

Amaziah was responsible for his own situation. He had done a wrong thing in hiring these mercenaries from apostate Israel; but when the wrong thing was pointed out to him, he was reluctant to turn aside from it, because to do so would incur some loss and unhappiness. So men, when they have started in a wrong course or have established themselves in a wrong attitude, make the still greater mistake of feeling that once they have started that way, they can hardly afford to change. Many a man might be a power instead of a spectator in his church, full of good works, a witness to others and a winner of souls; but he has associated himself with the world, with ungodly people, and even if at times he has a desire to do something of service to the kingdom of God, he turns away from the beautiful voice of that desire and says to himself, "No one now will expect any different kind of witness or life from me; and if I did make the change, it would mean a serious dislocation in my life and its habits, and I would have to give up some things to which I have become attached." So in all the areas of life can be heard the ring of those one hundred talents.

When great reforms are advocated, that is always the answer of the world and of self: "What shall we do for the one hundred talents? We cannot afford that loss." The state of Pennsylvania last year derived millions of dollars of revenue from its participation in the sale of strong drink. When objections are made, the answer is always the same—the one hundred talents. What shall we do for them? See what the state gets out of this tax: how many roads it builds, how many salaries it pays. So governments acquiesce in moral iniquity because of the revenue derived from it.

A noted West Virginia lawyer, close to the liquor situation in that state, told me how a friend of his on the board regulating the sale in that state could have made half a million dollars in a minute of time, and without any danger of legal reprisal if he had yielded to a proposal made to him. But he was one of those who put conscience and right above the one hundred talents. But for fear of the loss of popularity, favor, political influence, loss of money, or the giving up of sinful pleasure, men often prefer a little loss to deep and terrible and eternal spiritual loss.

DIVINE COMPENSATIONS

That was a great answer which the man of God rendered to the reluctant king who was so anxious about his one hundred talents. He said to him, "The Lord is able to give thee much more than this." And how true that is! What are one hundred talents to Almighty God? For the man who takes a stand for right and conscience there are always divine compensations. This is true oftentimes even in the things of this world. Honesty is always the best policy. It does not always bring a larger revenue than dishonesty. But in the long run it does. There is a world of meaning in that saying of Paul, "Godliness is profitable unto all things, having promise of the life that now is, and of that which is to come. This is a faithful saying and worthy of all acceptation." Godliness is a good investment, even from the standpoint of this world. When employers write for references about persons who have made application for some post, they never ask, for example: "Is he a young man who will have no objection to taking a drink now and then? Is she a young woman who has no scruples about going to a road house?" Instead of that they ask if the applicant's sobriety and honesty and virtue can be relied upon. Yes, even in the things of this world God is able to make good the one hundred talents. He is a good employer.

But there is another and a higher sense in which what the prophet said is forever true. Wherever a man loses anything, or any joy, or any part of this world for the sake of the kingdom of God, God knows how to compensate. "The Lord is able to give thee much more than this!" There are inner, spiritual riches of which the world knows nothing.

On one occasion the disciples came to Jesus after he had spoken to them about some of the demands of the kingdom of God and the sacrifices they must make. Peter, their spokesman, said, "Behold, we have forsaken all, and followed thee; what shall we have therefore?" You say we can't have riches; that that would keep us out of the kingdom of heaven. What then shall we have?

And Jesus answered, "Every one that hath forsaken houses, or brethren, or sisters, or father, or mother, or wife, or children, or lands, for my name's sake, shall receive an hundredfold, and shall inherit everlasting life."

Jesus was not telling them that if for his sake they had lost a house, they would get a hundred houses in return, or that if they had lost a hundred dollars, they would get ten thousand dollars in return, but that they would receive an hundredfold. Obedience to God introduces them to higher joys and higher possessions of which the world knows nothing. They get the most out of this life, and in the world to come "life everlasting."

Always Christ is telling us to keep our eye on that, on that life and on that world to come—for which this life and all its experiences are only an appointed trial or probation. Whenever, then, we are tempted to put the temporal above the eternal, the material above the spiritual, to think more about some financial or social or personal loss than about the voice of God and of conscience, we should remember the story of this ancient king who was troubled about the loss of one hundred talents, but to whom the prophet said, "God is able to give thee much more than this."

6

UNEXPECTED PROVIDENCE—
HAGAR

"Thou God seest me." (Genesis 16:13)

The glad cry of a woman who but a moment before was in despair and ready to die!

This is one of the great and familiar texts of the Bible. In any anthology of the Bible's greatest texts it would have to be included. Yet the popular use of the text in sermons is an interesting example of misuse and misinterpretation of Bible texts. In popular treatment the text has been used to remind and warn men that the eye of God is upon them when they enter into temptation and sin. "The eyes of the Lord run to and fro throughout the whole earth." This is an important truth; none more important. But it is not the primary truth of the text. When Hagar made this exclamation and named the very well where the angel had appeared unto her the "Well of the Living One Who Seeth Me," she was thinking of the kind and gracious providence of God. Until then, driven out of the camp of Abraham by the jealous Sarah, with not a friend near her to help or to sympathize with her, the poor bondwoman had thought she was forsaken. She was in despair. But to her glad surprise she discovered that God's eye was upon her and that his providence had followed her into the wilderness. This undoubtedly was what Hagar meant when she cried out, "Thou God seest me."

UNEXPECTED PROVIDENCE

However, since this verse through the ages has been piously and effectively used in the other sense, we shall first of all consider it this way: that God sees us in the sense that his eye is upon us—that there is nothing hid from his presence, and that he beholds our conduct.

GOD'S ALL-SEEING EYE

The eyes of God are upon us. The Bible has a great deal to say about the eyes of God. Some of the kings of Israel did that which was "right in the eyes of the Lord," and others did that which was "evil in the eyes of the Lord." "The eyes of the Lord run to and fro throughout the whole earth." "The eyes of the Lord are in every place, beholding the evil and the good." "His eyes are upon the ways of man." "His eyes were as a flame of fire."

If all men realized that the eye of God is upon them, a vast amount of evil would be left undone, and a vast amount of evil which has been done would be repented of. Herein is one of the great benefits of prayer. It makes us realize that we are in the view of God. That is what Christ meant when he said, "Watch and pray, that ye enter not into temptation." When they think they are unseen of their fellow men, or of some highly-esteemed friend, men will often do what they would be ashamed to do in the presence of others. Moses "looked this way and that way, and when he saw that there was no man, he slew the Egyptian, and hid him in the sand." Woodrow Wilson once related this incident concerning his godly father, Dr. Joseph R. Wilson, a noted Presbyterian minister. His father was once in a company of men who were having a heated discussion. In the midst of it one of them, not remembering that Dr. Wilson was present, let out a profane oath. Then seeing Dr. Wilson, he made an apology to him, saying, "Sir, I had forgotten that you were present. Please pardon me."

Whereupon Dr. Wilson replied, "It is not to me that you owe your apology, but to God."

God is always present. "Whither shall I go from thy spirit? or whither shall I flee from thy presence? If I ascend up into heaven, thou art there: if I make my bed in hell, behold, thou art there."

God sees us in our thoughts. Hence Paul tells us to bring "into captivity every thought to the obedience of Christ." Out of the heart, out of the imagination of the mind, flow the streams of our action. "As [a man] thinketh in his heart, so is he." There, first of all, men begin to fall. Let us guard, then, the chambers of our imagination and our thoughts, for God sees us. He tries the reins and searches the hearts of men.

God sees us in our acts and in our deeds. We are never hid from him. Victor Hugo's Jean Valjean in *Les Misérables* is a great sermon on the all-seeing eye of God. Under a new name the ex-convict had buried his past and had become the prosperous mayor of a provincial town. But one day he learned that in a neighboring village an old man who had been arrested for stealing apples had been identified as the notorious and long-sought ex-convict Jean Valjean. That news precipitated a crisis in the soul of Jean Valjean. Should he keep silent, or should he reveal his identity and then be sent back to the galleys with their dreadful slavery? Should he remain in paradise and become a demon, or go to hell and become an angel?

His first impulse was to say nothing. In order to hide his past he drew out of a secret closet a blue linen blouse, an old pair of trousers, a knapsack, and a huge cudgel, shod with iron at both ends. These were among the last ties which attached him to the Old Jean Valjean. He threw them into the fire. Then he seized the candlesticks which the bishop had given him and started to fling them into the flame. But as he did so, a voice said, "Jean Valjean! there shall be about you many voices . . . which will bless you; and one only. . . which will curse you in the darkness. . . . All these blessings shall fall before they reach Heaven; only the curse shall mount into the presence of God!"

When he heard that voice, realizing that the eye of God was upon him, Jean Valjean put the candlesticks back on the mantel and took the other articles out of the fire.

All through the night he fought his dreadful battle. When the morning came, he ordered his carriage and went to the courtroom. Just as the president of the court was about to pronounce sentence, the true ex-convict arose and said, "I am Jean Valjean."

God sees us not only in the hour of temptation, but in the hour of our transgressions and sins. "Thou God seest me." How men have found that out! And how they have tried in vain to hide from the face of God! What is conscience but the sense of God's eye upon us? How true to the great drama of human life is that scene in the garden of Eden where the man and the woman, having disobeyed God's command, tried in vain to hide themselves amid the trees of the garden.

In Dickens' powerful tale *Barnaby Rudge*, the evildoer confessed that for eight and twenty years the man whom he had slain had never changed and never disappeared. He was always there before him—in the dark night and in the sunshine; in the moonlight and in the twilight, in the light of the fire, in the lamp and the candle; in the gloom of winter; on sea and on land; on the quays and in the marketplace; in solitude and in the center of the busy crowd. Always he had been conscious of that terrible form towering above him with uplifted and avenging hand. O strange, mysterious, indefinable, inescapable conscience! "Thou God seest me!"

Let us hear again Psalm 139, "If I make my bed in hell behold, thou art there. . . . If I say, Surely the darkness shall cover me; even the night shall be light about me. Yea, the darkness hideth not from thee; but the night shineth as the day." In one of the old dramas dealing with Joseph and his temptation, when Joseph hesitated and drew back, the temptress said to him that she would throw her skirt over the face and head of the god whose image stood in her chamber, so that he would not be able to see their sin. But Joseph answered, "But my God sees!"'

GOD'S PROVIDENCE AND CARE

This is the primary and literal meaning of the words of Hagar, "Thou God seest me." She was not thinking of how God saw her in her temptations or in any evil, that she might have done, but how God was caring for her in that wilderness, in the hour of her sorrow and distress.

"Thou God seest me." That truth came to her with a glad and beautiful surprise. The poor slave girl had never doubted that God saw Abraham, or Sarah, who had driven her out from the tents of Abraham. But now she learned that God saw and cared for the outcast slave. "Thou God seest me." Be sure to put the emphasis on the me. It was that conviction and faith which gave her courage to go back to her hard lot at the encampment of Abraham.

Hagar had another, and subsequent, revelation of this great truth that God cared for her. When Isaac had been born to Sarah, Sarah drove Hagar and her child Ishmael away from Abraham's tents, out upon the blazing desert. The bread and water that Abraham had given her when she departed was soon exhausted, and the despairing Hagar laid her child down in what shade one of the desert bushes afforded. Then, in order that she might not see the death of her child, she flung herself down upon her face on the desert, a bowshot off, and lifted up her voice and wept. Again she heard the voice of the angel of God who said to her, "What aileth thee, Hagar? fear not; for God hath heard the voice of the lad. . . . Arise, lift up the lad, . . . for I will make him a great nation." Then "God opened her eyes, and she saw a well of water; and she went and filled the bottle with water, and gave the lad drink."

God opened Hagar's eyes in that desert place, and she saw the well of water in the very place where in her grief and despair a moment ago she was ready to perish. Here again we have an illustration of this great truth of God's providence, "Thou God seest me."

In my mother's diary is a passage written at the time of some trial in her life. This entry tells of how she was reading Mark's account of the storm on the Sea of Galilee, and how the disciples thought they were going to perish; but how Jesus, from the mountaintop where he had gone to pray, saw them "toiling in rowing." A beautiful expression that, of the sympathy and care of God. Whatever our distress, we can be sure that God sees us and that God cares for us. If ever we are tempted to cry out with the psalmist, "No man cared for my soul," let us remember that God cares for us and that his providence is over us. As Jeremy Taylor, that master of English style, once put it, "We are safer in God's storm, with God present, than we are in the calm of the world." Whatever our difficulties, let us have faith that God will open our eyes and that we shall see, as Hagar saw in the wildernes a well of water springing up for our refreshment. W can answer every temptation to doubt and despair, every assault of the world and of the Devil, with that beautiful confession of faith by the slave girl there in the lonely wilderness: "Thou God seest me."

7

THE MAN WHO CAME BY NIGHT—NICODEMUS

"The same came to Jesus by night." (John 3:2)

Night has fallen over Jerusalem, and only the faint, dim out line of its walls and towers and pinnacles is visible. Here, close to the wall of the city, is a garden. In this garden are costly tombs for the dead, for it is a burying place for the rich. But now stand aside, for here approach two men carrying a burden between them. The odor of myrrh and frankincense and cassia tells us that it is a body that they are carrying, embalmed for the tomb. Now for a moment they stop to rest, gently laying their burden down and anxiously looking about as if some foe might appear to interfere with their sacred and tender mission. At length they come to the door of a notable sepulcher, plainly that of a rich man, although the man whose body they bear had not on earth whereon to lay his head.

One of the two men pushes open the great stone door which swings easily on its pivot. Then down the steps they bear their precious burden and deposit it in the innermost recess. Silently they stand for a little in affectionate contemplation and sorrowful reverence. The old, old fashion; the old, old grief that has been in the world since Abel died; the pain of separation from our friends, which will be here until the grave gives up its dead and the sea hers. Then the two men ascend the steps, roll the great door shut, and depart. Let us bow down in wonder and adoration, for this is the Redeemer's body that these men have laid in that tomb

Now comes another, and an earlier, night scene. This time it is the Mount of Olives, the favorite resort and refuge of the Son of Man. Below are the valley of Kedro and, rising in the distance, the ramparts of Jerusalem These olive trees on another night will echo the Savior's groans and sighs. The very soil on which he sits with his disciples will, on that night, be crimsoned with his bloody sweat. But this night all is quiet and peace. The Master sits discoursing of the kingdom of God with his twelve disciples about him. Now up the slope of Olivet comes a solitary man. At once the disciples are on the alert. As the man comes nearer, they note by his robe and dress that he is a Pharisee, and therefore an enemy of their Master. In belligerent mood Peter and some of the others start forward to repel the stranger. But Christ, bidding them refrain, says, "Peace! This man comes not as a foe, but as a friend." Then speaking to the stranger he says, "Friend, thou doctor of the law, come hither, and sit here by my side. What brings thee this night to my place of prayer and meditation?"

The stranger is Nicodemus, who came first, and came last, to Jesus by night, a ruler among the Jews. He and Jesus have the following conversation:

Nicodemus: "Master, we know that thou art a teacher come from God: for no man can do these miracles that thou doest except God be with him."

Jesus: "Verily, verily, I say unto thee, Except a man be born again, he cannot see the kingdom of God."

Nicodemus: "How can a man be born when he is old? Can he enter the second time into his mother's womb and be born ?"

Jesus: "That which is born of the flesh is flesh; and that which is born of the Spirit is spirit. Marvel not that I say unto thee, Ye must be born again."

Nicodemus: "How can this be?"

Jesus: "The wind bloweth where it listeth, and thou hearest the sound thereof, but canst not tell whence it cometh or whither it goeth: so is every one that is born of the Spirit."

Nicodemus: "How can these things be?"

Jesus: "Art thou a master of Israel and knowest not these things? Art thou a teacher in the things of God, and yet knowest not the first and the last great fact of the spiritual life? This, Nicodemus, this truth of the new birth, is not a fact that men know or learn naturally. No man has gone up to heaven to discover this truth, but I alone, the Son of Man, who has come down from heaven, can teach it. As Moses lifted up the serpent in the wilderness, even so must I, the Son of Man, be lifted up; that just as the smitten people of Israel, bitten with the serpents, looked upon that brazen serpent and were healed, so whosoever looketh and believeth on me might have eternal life. For God so loved the world, Nicodemus, that he gave his only begotten Son, that whosoever believeth in him should not perish but have everlasting life. For God sent not his Son into the world to condemn the world; but that the world through him might be saved."

Over the rest of that marvelous nocturnal interview the Holy Spirit has drawn the curtain; but that night, we doubt not, Nicodemus was born again and entered the kingdom of heaven. In that wonderful night interview there first fell upon human ears that great saying, so sweet and simple that you can teach it to the youngest child, yet so profound that the greatest intellects have pondered over it; a saying into the meaning of which the angels themselves desire to look; that saying which sums up the' length and breadth and the height and depth of the Christian faith; that saying that will be the song of the redeemed in heaven—"God so loved the world, that he gave his only begotten Son, that whosoever believeth in him should not perish, but have everlasting life."

THE NEW BIRTH

One of the stars which shone in the sky of this night when Nicodemus talked with Christ is the fact, and the mystery, of the new birth. Dwight L. Moody used to speak of his two birthdays, the day on which he was born in East Northfield, Massachusetts, and the day on which he was "born again" at Boston. That was the day his Sunday school teacher, Edward Kimball, put his hand upon his shoulder and said, "Dwight, don't you think it is time for you to give your heart to the Lord?" It was time, indeed! It was "the tenth hour" for him; but at that hour he gave his heart to Christ and entered into the kingdom of heaven. Near the end of his life Moody wrote:

Some morning you will read in the papers that D. L. Moody is dead. Don't believe a word of it! At that moment I shall be more alive than I am now. I shall have gone up higher, that is all; out of this old clay tenement into a house that is immortal, a body that sin cannot touch, that sin cannot taint, a body fashioned like unto his glorious body. I was born of the flesh in 1837. I was born of the Spirit in 1856. That which is born of the flesh may die; that which is born of the Spirit shall live forever.

The change in one's life and heart which is necessary before one can enter the kingdom of heaven is just the same as that to which Christ referred on another occasion. Taking up a little child, he said to his disciples, who were disputing as to place and rank in the kingdom of heaven, "Except ye be converted, and become as little children, ye shall not enter into the kingdom of heaven."

Christ said that this work of regeneration is secret. You can hear the wind, but cannot see it. But you can see the effect of the wind as it tosses the branches of the trees, or agitates the sea with great waves, or drives the clouds through the heavens. So, although we cannot see the process of the new birth, we can see the effects of it, and we can feel the effects of it. When a man has experienced this spiritual change, upon which no one can put his hand any more than one can put his hand on the wind, he is made into a new creature. As George Whitefield, a great preacher of the new birth who turned thousands upon thousands to God, put it:

> As a piece of gold that was once in the ore, after it has been purified and polished is a new piece, and as a bright glass that has been covered with filth and then wiped, so that it becomes transparent and clear, is a new glass; and as the flesh of Naaman, when he was recovered of his leprosy, came again like unto the flesh of a little child, and he could be spoken of as a new man; so our souls, although still the same as to essence, when they are purged, purified and cleansed from their natural dross, filth and leprosy, by the blessed influence of the Holy Spirit can be truly said to be made anew.

There is no more important question than this, Am I a truly converted man? Have I been born again? This question is important and vital because Christ said that we must be born again. Just as imperfections of the body do not deny one's physical birth, so imperfections of character do not deny the new birth. Yet there are certain fruits and signs which bear witness to the new birth and the new life. One is love to our fellow men. So John says that if we love the brethren, we know that we have passed from death to life. Another sign of the new birth is love toward God, as expressed in faith in Christ and his atonement on the cross. Only a regenerate man can glory in the cross of Christ. How striking and significant it is that in this great interview in which Jesus spoke of the new birth, he concluded his sermon to Nicodemus by speaking of the Cross. Only by faith in Christ crucified can men be redeemed, for, he said, looking forward to his atoning death on the cross, "As Moses lifted up the serpent in the wilderness, even so must the Son of man be lifted up: that whosoever believeth in him should not perish, but have eternal life."

THE FRUIT OF THE SPIRIT

The gift of faith is definitely a gift of the Holy Spirit. But the Holy Spirit also shows his presence, his power, and the reality of the new birth, by what the apostle Paul calls "the fruit of the Spirit." He says, "Walk in the Spirit, and ye shall not fulfill the lust of the flesh. For the flesh lusteth against the Spirit, and the Spirit against the flesh: and these are contrary the one to the other." Then, after enumerating some of the evil works of the flesh—such as impurity, strife, envy, drunkenness, and murder—the fruit of the Spirit is love, joy, peace, longsuffering, he gives his celebrated list of the fruit of the Spirit: "But gentleness, goodness, faith, meekness, temperance [self-control]: against such there is no law. . . . If we live in the Spirit, let us also walk in the Spirit." There Paul says, practically, what James says in connection with faith and works: "Show me thy faith without thy works, and I will show thee my faith by my works."

When he mentions the new birth, Peter speaks along the same line as Paul. "Ye were not redeemed," Peter writes, "with corruptible things, as silver and gold, from your vain conversation. . . but with the precious blood of Christ, as of a lamb without blemish and without spot." Then he speaks of the evidence of the new birth and the presence of the Holy Spirit in the believer's life: "Seeing ye have purified your souls in obeying the truth through the Spirit unto unfeigned love of the brethren, see that ye love one another with a pure heart fervently: being born again, not of corruptible seed, but of incorruptible, by the word of God, which liveth and abideth for ever."

It is the Spirit of God which makes us able to be "partakers of the divine nature." When he speaks of that change, Peter lists his beautiful rosary, as it were, of the Christian virtues which blossom in the life of one who through the Holy Spirit and the new birth has passed from death unto life:

> And beside this, giving all diligence, add to your faith virtue; and to virtue knowledge; and to knowledge temperance [self-control]; and to temperance patience; and to patience godliness; and to godliness brotherly kindness; and to brotherly kindness charity. For if these things be in you, and abound, they make you that ye shall neither be barren nor unfruitful in the knowledge of our Lord Jesus Christ.

We ought, then, to think often about the "fruit of the Spirit." We ought to lament and repent if we see no sign of these virtues or fruits in our lives, and earnestly pray to the Holy Spirit to do his gracious work in our hearts.

When Nicodemus went to Jesus that first night, there is no doubt that he was interested in eternal life. But in one respect there was a great difference between him and that other ruler, the rich young man who came to Jesus and asked, "What must I do to inherit eternal life?" That ruler came boldly by day before all the people on the street and bowed down before Jesus; whereas Nicodemus came by night, undoubtedly for the same reason that Joseph of Arimathea had not avowed himself a disciple of Jesus, that is, "for fear of the Jews."

We know, however, that the Holy Spirit reaped the seed which he had sown that night in the heart of Nicodemus; for this is shown later on at a meeting of the Sanhedrin. The officers who had been sent to seize Jesus and bring him before the chief priests and Pharisees reported to the Sanhedrin without their prisoner. The chief priests and the Pharisees said to them, "Why have ye not brought him?"

The officers answered, "Never man spake like this man."

Whereupon the chief priests and the Pharisees scornfully said to their officers: "Are ye also deceived? Have any of the rulers or of the Pharisees believed on him?"

Nicodemus, as a ruler of the synagogue, was present at this meeting of the Sanhedrin. This question of the Pharisees and priests, "Have any of the rulers believed on him?" touched his heart and awakened deep emotions. He might have kept silent; but he spoke up and said, "Doth our law judge any man, before it hear him, and know what he doeth?"

Whereupon the chief priests and Pharisees said to him, and, no doubt, with an accent of mingled amazement and contempt: "Art thou also of Galilee? Search, and look: for out of Galilee ariseth no prophet."

From this incident we know that Nicodemus, although he did not openly confess that he was a follower of Jesus, at least had the courage to say that Jesus ought not to be condemned as an impostor without a hearing. But at the very last Nicodemus came out into the light as an open believer in Jesus. John tells us, after he has related how Joseph of Arimathea besought Pilate that he might take away the body of Jesus, that "there came also Nicodemus, which at the first came to Jesus by night, and brought a mixture of myrrh and aloes, about an hundred pound weight. Then took they the body of Jesus, and wound it in linen clothes with the spices, as the manner of the Jews is to bury."

Nicodemus, who first came to Jesus by night and heard that wonderful truth of the new birth, had at length been born again!

8

RETRIBUTION IN KIND—
ADONI-BEZEK

"And cut off his thumbs and his great toes." (Judges 1:6)

A woman once said to a French cardinal, "My lord cardinal, God does not pay at the end of every week; nevertheless, he pays."

This is a rough-and-tumble world that we enter when we open the Bible at the book of Judges. Men are a law unto themselves, and the result is lawlessness and anarchy. Everything is on the heroic scale: mirth, sorrow, revenge, hate, murder, anger, and love of country. Silhouetted against this dark background are strange and unforgettable characters who move across the stage of Israel to the music of strong passions—Samson, Gideon, Jephthah, Jotham, and this monster of cruelty with whom the book commences, Adoni-bezek.

Adoni-bezek was a prince who ruled in one of the strongholds of the Canaanites, a stronghold as yet untaken at the time of the death of Joshua. This monster amused himself with the savage mutilation of the princes whom he conquered in battle, cutting off their thumbs and their great toes, thus rendering them unfit for military service. To cruelty and mutilation he added insult and degradation by compelling them to grovel about his table in the palace, where he threw crusts of bread to them as if they were a pack of dogs. But at length his day came. Simeon and Judah and their men at war took his stronghold and put his people to death. But Adoni-bezek himself they reserved for a more poetic justice and grim retribution. They dealt with him just as he had dealt with the princes who were unfortunate enough to fall into his hands. They mutilated him just as he had mutilated his own victims. When he had suffered this mutilation, Adoni-besek exclaimed, "As I have done, so the Lord hath requited me."

The incident is a striking example of the judgments of God. Sometimes justice seems to go on slow foot, and we wonder if there is such a thing as justice in the world, so tardy and ofttimes invisible are its decrees. But at other times justice amazes us and startles us with the flashing of its sword. Just as on a close, heavy day a flash of lightning clears the atmosphere and makes the heavens luminous, so a flash of God's justice makes luminous the spiritual firmament and restores to us our faith in the moral ordering of the world. For long years this brutal prince practiced his infamous atrocities, till he had almost a hundred mutilated men groveling at his table. He was secure in his stronghold; it seemed that he would never be called to account. When the blow fell, it came from this unexpected quarter, two of the tribes who had come up out of Egypt, Judah and Simeon. The record is that they "found Adoni-bezek in Bezek: and they fought against him." So men's iniquities find them out. If not today, then tomorrow; and if not tomorrow, then the day after tomorrow.

But there is something more in this ancient confession, wrung from the lips of agony, "As I have done, so the Lord hath requited me." What this sets before us is not only the fact of God's retributive justice, but the manner of it; not only that God pays, but how he pays. There is a correspondence between the transgression and the punishment. This is strikingly brought out in those words of Paul to the Colossians, "The wrong that a man doeth—that wrong he shall receive again." This translation is strictly in keeping with the original, and much more arresting than what we read in the King James Version, "He that doeth wrong shall receive for the wrong which he hath done." This states not only the certainty of retribution, but that there is a mysterious and inexorable connection between the wrong that is done and the punishment inflicted. In other words, a man's sins come back to him. The wrong that he does, that wrong he gets again, if not in actual reduplication, always in effect and principle. The Greeks used to speak of the "retribution of Neoptolemos." Neoptolemos had slain Priam at an altar, and at an altar Neoptolemos himself was slain. So in Hebrew theology and history is "the retribution of Adoni-bezek."

There are other unforgettable exhibitions of this in the Bible, aside from this grim story of the Judges. One day Jacob put goatskins on his arms and hands, and came into his old father, Isaac, whose eyes were set with age. Pretending that he was Esau, he fraudulently got his father's blessing, the blessing of the first-born. The years passed, and one day Simeon and Levi and Judah and Issachar and the rest of them, the sons of Jacob, came to the patriarch's encampment. They held up before him a coat of many colors, all spotted and dappled with blood. They told him, although he knew without their telling him, that it was the coat of Joseph, the coat of many colors, and that a wild beast must have killed him. "Know now," they said, "whether this is thy son's coat or not."

And he knew it and said, "It is my son's coat. An evil beast hath devoured him. Joseph is without doubt torn to pieces." All his sons and his daughters rose up to comfort him; but he refused to be comforted, and said, "I will go down to Sheol, to the grave, to my son, sorrowing."

The old man's deception had come back to him. He deceived his father, and his sons in turn deceived him. As he had done, so the Lord had requited him.

David's Retribution

David is another example of this manner of God's punishments. In the midst of his reign he committed murder and adultery. He repented of his sin, and was greatly forgiven. Yet, as the prophet Nathan told him when he announced his forgiveness, the sword never departed from his house. David lived to see the day when his own crimes, murder and adultery, were reproduced in his own sons, Amnon and Absalom. When Absalom drove David from his capital, after defiling his harem, and Shimei, standing on the highway as the fugitive king fled to the country across the Jordan, cursed David, saying, "Begone, begone, thou man of blood, thou base fellow," one of David's men-at-arms, Abishai, protested, and said to David, "Why should this dead dog curse my lord the king? Let me go over, I pray thee, and take off his head." But David responded, "What have I to do with you?. . . Behold, my son who came forth from my bowels, seeketh my life: how much more now may this Benjaminite do it. Let him alone, and let him curse; for the Lord hath bidden him." In his tribulations David recognized the exact and appropriate justice of God.

In his history of the French Revolution, Carlyle tells of a minister of the crown, Foulon, who, in objection to some proposed measure, was asked, "What will the people do?"

He exclaimed: "Let the people eat grass!"

When the Bastille fell, the mob did not forget the cruel jibe of this minister, "Let the people eat grass!" He was hanged from a post, "and his mouth after death was filled with grass, amid sounds as of Tophet, from a grass-eating people. Surely, if Revenge is a 'kind of Justice,' it is a 'wild' kind. . . . They that would make grass be eaten do now eat grass, in this manner? After long, dumb-groaning generations, has the turn suddenly become thine?"

A FATHER'S RETRIBUTION

At a Pennsylvania bankers' convention one of the bankers related an incident in the life of a judge whom he knew. In his college days he had been addicted to drink. Now he had a fine and promising son in college. Complaints soon reached him of his son's misbehavior—his drinking and general dissipation. The father called the son before him and remonstrated with him. He told the boy that he was ruining his prospects, and that his conduct would break his mother's heart.

Imagine his surprise when his son replied, "Why, father, they tell me you did just the same thing when you were at college." This flash of retributive justice in the words of his wayward son was, in the providence of God, the means of a radical transformation in the life of that father.

SATAN'S RETRIBUTION

That like produces like is a spiritual, no less than a natural, law. Sin is often punished in the very shape and fashion of the sin.

Milton in *Paradise Lost* describes how Satan, having deceived and tempted man in the guise of a serpent, returned to his capital where the leaders of the fallen angels had prepared a great feast in his honor. Satan recounted to them how in the form of a serpent he had tempted man and accomplished his ruin. Then he paused, expecting to hear a shout of applause, but what he heard instead was a "dismal universal hiss." Satan and all his angels had been turned into serpents. He had been punished in the form in which he sinned.

> He wondered, but not long
> Had leisure, wondering at himself now more.
> His visage drawn he felt too sharp and spare,
> His arms clung to his ribs, his legs entwining
> Each other, till, supplanted, down he fell,
> A monstrous serpent on his belly prone,
> Reluctant, but in vain; a greater power
> Now ruled him, punished in the shape he sinned,
> According to his doom.

OUR RETRIBUTION

We need not expect that we shall see very often such striking and unmistakable illustrations of this law of requital and recompense. Yet we can be sure that this principle of God's law is always silently at work. If a man lies and deceives another, his lie comes back to him. He may not be deceived in exactly the same way, but because he himself has lied and deceived, he cannot put his trust in anyone. The man who lives selfishly, as if he were the only one whose interests are to be considered, is punished by being left alone. Selfishness and egotism isolate and separate. There is no man so lonely as the selfish man.

The man who breaks the seventh commandment, commits adultery, and takes what is not his, at once puts himself in a position where he cannot trust any man or any woman, and will always be in fear for his own sacred possessions. The young man and the young woman who are loose and easy in their relationships, at once lose mutual respect and self-respect, and can put confidence in no affection because they regard it through the discolored glass of their own conduct.

We hear much today of the flouting and abandonment of what used to be considered the "standards" of conduct under the plea of self-expression. It is just as well to remember that however these standards are accepted or abandoned, honored or ridiculed, the laws of God, exact and inexorable in their recompense, go forward, doing their appointed work and registering their decrees. Today, tomorrow, and tonight, under the noise of the confusion of daily living, pause for a moment, and you will hear speaking that "still small voice," and you will see working those laws of compensation and recompense.

Some miles south of the harbor of Arbroath, Scotland, on the German Ocean, is the Bell Rock Light, built by the Scottish engineer Thomas Stevenson, grandfather of Robert Louis Stevenson. In olden times the abbot of the monastery at Arbroath had put up a bell on this dangerous reef to warn the incoming vessels. A pirate once sacked the town and sank the bell in the sea. The absence of this bell caused the wreck and destruction of many a vessel. Years afterward this same brigand of the sea on a stormy night was beating in toward Arbroath. He listened in vain for the bell on the reef which would give him his bearings, and he and his company went down with the ship to an ocean grave. "As I have done, so the Lord hath requited me."

It is to be noted here that Adoni-besek acquiesced in the severe judgment which had overtal:en him. In the savage punishment meted out to him by the Hebrew tribesmen he recognized the exact equivalent of what he himself had done. Nowhere in the Bible when God's judgment falls upon an evildoer does the evildoer himself protest against the judgment. On the contrary he acquiesces in it, as did this mutilated king, and as the thief on the cross did when he said, "We receive the due reward of our deeds." If there is a state of future retribution—and if we believe in God and in the Bible and in Christ, there is such a state it is well to remember that there will be no complaints against the judgments of God. It is only in the mind of speculation that such questions or doubts arise. The objections to future punishment will be confined to this present world, and even then they will not come from the lips of those who have received the due reward of their deeds.

GOOD DEEDS ALSO COME BACK

This truth, that the wrong a man hath done he shall receive again, draws its own conclusions and preaches its own sermon. But, happily, there is a brighter, more hopeful, and a more pleasing side to this truth. If a man's evil deeds come back to him, so also his good deeds come back to him. Christ made that plain when he said, "All things whatsoever ye would that men should do to you, do ye even so to them." And in his apocalypse of the day of judgment he tells of those who will be surprised by the resurrection of the good they did in this world.

However warned we may be by the other side of this truth, we should have no doubt as to this, that the bread which we cast upon the waters one day will return to us. Truth, purity, compassion, tenderness, loyalty, faith—all these things are their own reward. Neither life nor death, nor angels nor principalities, nor things present nor things to come, shall be able to separate a man from them. The prophet said of him who did no wrong, but whose divine life was filled with righteousness and good deeds—although that life came to an end in this world amid clouds of execration, obloquy, agony, and shame—"He shall see of the travail of his soul, and shall be satisfied." What is true of Christ will be true of every faithful disciple who bears his cross and follows in his steps.

The good that a man does is sure to come back to him. Therefore in the morning sow thy seed, and in the evening withhold not thy hand. In due time we shall reap if we faint not. Yes, we shall reap! We reap in the blessings of a good conscience, in the gratitude and friendship of those whom we have helped, in the "well done" of our own conscience, and in the fellowship of the just made perfect in the life which is to come.

9

WEAK MOMENTS—ESAU

"For one morsel of pottage." (Hebrews 12:16)

Isaac and Rebecca had two boys, Easu and Jacob, and they were as unlike as two boys often are, though children of the same father and of the same mother, and brought up in the same home and environment. Isaac loved Esau, although he knew that the promises centered about Jacob; whereas Rebecca loved Jacob. Jacob was of a meditative cast of mind, spending his time about the home and with his mother; Esau was a rough, bluff, hearty sort of fellow, fond of outdoor sports and exercises, and a mighty hunter.

This particular day Esau had been out over the hills on a hunting expedition. He had been pursuing the swift antelope, the roebuck, and the stag. Now, with his trophies thrown over his shoulder, he was returning from the hunt, coming faint and weary and hungry into the encampment of his father, Isaac. When he was still a little distance from the camp, his nostrils caught the odor of the pottage which Jacob was cooking. Smelling the savory pottage, Esau said to his brother Jacob, "Feed me, I pray thee, with that same red pottage; for I am faint!"

The crafty Jacob saw his opportunity to take advantage of the greed and hunger of his brother. He told him that he would give him to eat of the pottage upon condition that Esau sold him his birthright. But just now Esau was not thinking about the birthright or his future. All that he wanted just now was to satisfy his hunger with the pottage which Jacob was cooking. "What profit," he said, "shall this birthright do to me?" Who cares anything about that, or the future? I am about to die with hunger. Take the birthright, if you want it, only let me have the pottage, and let me have it now! So he swore to Jacob, and then Jacob gave him the pottage. "And he did eat and. drink, and rose up, and went his way: thus Esau despised his birthright."

This incident in the life of Esau reveals the danger of a man's weak moments, and warns us of how much can be thrown away in a single moment, never again to be recovered.

THE STRENGTH OF THAT WEAKEST MOMENT

You can hardly say that Esau was a man of mere sensuality, who had no appreciation at all of the birthright or the blessing. That cannot have been so, for we read afterward of the bitter remorse that seized him because he had once despised his birthright, and how carefully and with tears he besought Isaac to give it back to him. He was not a man of pronounced and uninterrupted materialism and animalism, but a man who in the temptation of a moment threw away his birthright. He was just as strong as that weak moment when he became hungry and thirsty from the fields and smelled the pottage of his brother. A chain is just as strong as the weakest link in it. A man's character is just as strong as the weakest link in it. It is arresting and solemnizing to remember that in the last analysis we are judged and tested, not by our excellencies, not by our so-called strong points, but by our weak points. The real trial will be the trial and test of your weak place and your weak moment. A battle line is just as strong as the weakest point or place in the whole length of the line.

On the second day of the great battle of Chickamauga, September 20, 1863, General Rosecrans, having received a mistaken report that there was a gap between two divisions in the center of his line, sent an order to General Wood to close up on General Reynolds. There was another division between Wood and Reynolds; but, obedient to the order, Wood took his division out of the line and marched it to the rear to join the division of General Reynolds. This left a great gap in the Union line of battle. Immediately the veteran corps of Longstreet, who had been sent from Lee's army in Virginia to reinforce Bragg, smashed through that opening and drove the center and right wing of the Union Army from the field. Complete disaster was averted only by the heroic stand of Thomas at the other end of the line. The Union battle line was just as strong as that place in the center where a division had been withdrawn. The battle line of a man's life is just as strong as the weakest place in that line.

The tempter knows our weak places, and those places are where he assails us. Satan did not come to Jesus and ask him to turn stones into bread on the first day, but on the fortieth day, when Jesus was hungry. Jacob did not come with his infamous proposal to Esau to barter his birthright when Esau was starting out for the field after a full breakfast. He did not make it the night before or the day following. But he made it just at the time that Esau came in faint and hungry. Esau's hunger gave Jacob his opportunity.

SOME OF OUR WEAK MOMENTS

1. A weak moment is often caused by bodily appetite and passions. It was so with Esau. When his nostrils dilated with the savor of the red pottage, he was willing in the passion of his hunger to sell his birthright for a taste of the savory stew. It was a natural, but an animal, appetite and passion. How many since Esau, tempted in such a moment, tempted in the appetites or desires of the body, have done themselves irreparable injury and mortgaged their future. Noble and gifted souls in a single moment have cast themselves into the thralldom of Satan because they forgot the future and said to themselves, "I am about to die. I must satisfy this appetite."

Every man is of the earth, earthy; and first is that which is natural. Suddenly and in an unexpected moment the fires of appetite burst out of the furnace of a man's nature. When the flames once begin to burn, they will have everything in sight. All past resolves, all holy memories, all righteous fears, all hopes and expectations, all aspirations after a godly life, may not suffice to bind again the beast that has broken loose within the breast of man. You may talk to such a man about tomorrow, and he will laugh in your face. "Tomorrow, with its unknown and hypothetical pleasures, what is that to me, compared with the present? Let me eat; let me satisfy this appetite. That is the great thing; that is the only concern of the present."

Paul once said that he kept the body under, lest, having preached to others, he himself should become a castaway. A solemn verse that is. If a man like Paul—so devoted, so self-denying, so beaten and buffeted with the storms of life—made a testimony like that, what must we do! How does it behoove you and me by prayer and watching and vigilance to keep the body under.

When he realized what he had done, Esau cried out with an exceeding great and bitter cry. Oh, how often that cry has been raised; through how many homes, in the chambers of how many lives, its echoes have flung themselves from wall to wall! In a moment, for one morsel of pottage, for a gratification that was gone ere it was consummated, a man has sold his birthright, put himself under the bondage of fear and shame, and inflicted a wound which time itself will not be able to heal.

2. Another weak moment is the moment when a man's greed or avarice is excited and stirred. Just for the fear of losing a few dollars or for the sake of making a few more dollars, men will compromise with evil, will break their pledged word and put a stain upon their conscience. When we see what it will persuade some men to do, and how it can enkindle hate and venom in the heart of man, we realize what the inspired writer is talking about when he says that the love of money is the root of all evil.

At the end of the season the owner of a ranch in Colorado for whom I worked one summer went to deliver a load of baled alfalfa hay to a gentleman in the city of Denver. He had asked for what is called "second cutting," the best. While we were depositing the bales in his barn, the customer came out and inspected some of the hay. Then he said to the owner of the ranch, "This is not second cutting."

The ranch owner was silent for a moment and then, with an air of injured honor, said, "This is what you asked for, is it not?"

The ranchman was a good man, a Christian man, but he had had a profitless summer. He never intended to lie or cheat; but when he saw a few dollars slipping out of his grasp if he told the truth, he told the lie. In a weak moment he had cheated and defrauded and lied.

3. The moment of fear is a weak moment for some people. A man who could face a cannonade without tremor or could storm a fortress without faltering, will flinch before the pointed finger of scorn. Peter was in many respects a brave man. When the mob

appeared in the garden with swords and staves, Peter drew out his own sword and smote off the ear of the servant of the high priest. But just a little while afterward, as he sat by the fire warming himself, a serving maid pointed a finger at him and said, "Art not thou also one of this man's disciples?" and Peter with an oath denied that he ever knew his Lord.

THE INEVITABLE AND BITTER REMORSE

Esau's great and bitter cry, it is true, came after he had found that Jacob had cheated him out of the blessing and that his father now could not change his mind or revoke the blessing. But the writer of the letter to the Hebrews, when he says that Esau "found no place of repentance, though he sought it carefully with tears," definitely associates his loss of the blessing with his former scorn of his birthright: "For ye know how that afterward, when he would have inherited the blessing, he was rejected: for he found no place of repentance, though he sought it carefully with tears." By a base and wicked fraud Jacob, at Rebekah's suggestion, had cheated Esau out of the blessing. But the hand of God was in that act of deception, and Esau's bitter cry, when he found that he had lost the blessing, had in it a deep echo of remorse because he must have realized that his scorning of the birthright and selling it for a mess of pottage made him unworthy of the blessing. There has not been a man in all the history of the world who has succeeded in beating the moral system—not one who betrayed himself and bartered his birthright who did not one day have to utter that bitter cry of lament and remorse.

Esau said, "What profit shall this birthright do to me?"

Christ answered his question, "What shall it profit a man if he shall gain the whole world, and lose his own soul? or what shall a man give in exchange for his soul?" It was easy for Esau in a moment to trade the blessing for a mess of pottage; but it was impossible, even with tears, to find it again.

> And is there in God's world so drear a place
> Where the loud bitter cry is raised in vain?
> Where tears of penance come too late for grace,
> As on th' uprooted flower the genial rain?

Watch by our father Isaac's pastoral door—
The birthright sold, the blessing lost and won,
Tell, Heaven has wrath that can relent no more,
The Grave, dark deeds that cannot be undone.

We barter life for pottage; sell true bliss
For wealth or power, for pleasure or renown;
Thus, Esau-like, our Father's blessing miss,
Then wash with fruitless tears our faded crown.[1]

Perhaps someone will catch an echo of that bitter cry of Esau and will hesitate and will be persuaded to stop and reflect before he casts away that which can never be reclaimed. Christ tells us to watch and to pray. What he said to the sleeping disciples is true of you and me, "The spirit indeed is willing, but the flesh is weak."

Beware, then, of a weak moment. Irreparable injury can be done to a life in such a moment. The best defense for such moments and for such temptations is the companionship of Jesus Christ. If our faith and trust is in him, if we are in his fellowship, then it will be with us as it was with that mighty warrior Paul, who said when the grace of Christ was with him, "When I am weak, then I am strong."

---

1. John Keble, *The Christian Year*.

10

A TOMB WITHOUT A TENANT—ABSALOM

"Now Absalom in his lifetime had taken and reared up for himself a pillar, which is in the king's dale." (2 Samuel 18:18)

On the battlefield of Saratoga stands a towering obelisk commemorative of that decisive struggle of the American Revolution. About its base are four deep niches, and in these are bronze figures of the generals who commanded there. In the first stands Horatio Gates; in the second, Schuyler; and in the third, Morgan. But the fourth, alas! stands empty. The soldier who won that niche of fame has forfeited his right to be remembered. Below the empty niche cut in the stone there is a solitary name. As the eye falls upon it, a vision rises: I see a young Colonial officer leading his troops on a wintry morning against the battlements of Quebec. Again, I see him charging the British lines at Saratoga; and yet again, crouching at the midnight hour by the murmuring Hudson, bartering his soul to Satan. The scene changes. I see a lonely room in London, and an old man dying—friendless, homeless, godless—Benedict Arnold, hero, patriot, traitor.

Here is another beautiful, but unoccupied, monument. The history of Absalom closes with one of those overwhelming contrasts in which the Bible delights. When Joab had thrust the three darts through his body, Absalom was cut down from the limb of the oak tree where he had been caught by his luxuriant hair, and cast into the nearest pit. As the companies of soldiers marched by on their way back from the battlefield, each man took a stone and cast it upon Absalom until a great mound of boulders marked the last resting place of that rebel prince.

In strange contrast with this lonely and rude seplucher was the costly pillar or mausoleum which Absalom had reared for himself in the king's dale. That was the tomb which he had expected to occupy. There his flawless body, arrayed in royal robes and prepared for the sepulcher with spikenard and ointment, was to be laid away with an empire's lamentation. It would be a memorial to his greatness, and men of succeeding generations would tarry by the tomb and say, "Here lies Absalom, the son of David."

How different was the grave into which he was cast like a dead dog! Instead of resting in a marble mausoleum, that flawless body—once without a blemish from the sole of his foot to the crown of his head—lay gashed and broken at the bottom of the forest pit, covered with a heap of stones, and with not a soul, save his brokenhearted father, to mourn over him. But yonder in the king's dale stood his pillar. The rising sun gilded with glory its precious stones and silver and gold. The noonday sun halted to behold its beauty; and night draped its white shaft with her ethereal robe. But it was a tomb without an occupant, a pillar without a hero, a monument without a man.

The stone pile and the pillar! Absalom was not the only man who planned for a pillar and ended beneath a stone pile. There are many young Absaloms of today with ambitious hopes and daring plans who wish to make a name for themselves and win a high place in the world. A large number of them will fail. Their end will be a stone pile of regret or infamy, instead of the pillar of true fame. If we leave fame out of it altogether, many of those who plan to be useful and honorable men and women in their day will never reach that goal. What are some of the reasons why they will fail?

The Lack of a Purpose

Robert Burns wrote of himself: "The great misfortune of my life was to want an aim." To that want he attributed many of the misfortunes which overtook him in life.

With a heart completely tinder and eternally lighted up by some goddess or other, a wild logical talent, a strong appetite for sociability and a native hilarity and a constitutional melancholy which made him flee solitude, he lacked the balance wheel of a definite and high aim, and many sorrows and much heaviness of heart were the results.

When a man has some well-defined end at which he wishes to arrive, that purpose acts as a stimulant upon his mind, stirs latent talent within him, collects and marshals his wandering powers and concentrates them upon the one chief work to be done. There are thousands of young persons drifting aimlessly about, just waiting for the breath of the wind of a high purpose to stir them into action and surprise them with the powers that lie slumbering in their souls. When a high purpose takes possession of a man, he has a defense against the inroads of vicious habits which waste his powers and undermine his manhood. The tempter finds it difficult to gain the ear of that man who has set his face steadfastly toward some worthy end and is bending all his energy to secure that end. It is the company of such a purpose that enables a man to endure hardness, cheers him in any moment of depression, and makes him capable of those sacrifices and self-denials without which no man can succeed.

The easy and incontrovertible proof of this is the story of those men who won distinction in one or another of the fields of human enterprise. Napoleon is not a model for any man. Yet in the power of a purpose, and in readiness to sacrifice to that purpose, he is. As a student in the military schools he gave himself to his studies, aiming at distinction in military life, and separated himself from those companions whose habits interfered with his purpose.

Let us take another field. *Paradise Lost* and the "Hymn on the Morning of the Nativity of Christ" were not accidental productions. They were not, as Milton says, "the result of the trencher fury of a rhyming parasite." The man who wrote them tells us how he labored for such excellence:

> I began thus far to assent both to them and divers of my friends here at home, and not less to an inward prompting, which now grew daily upon me, that by labor and intense study, which I take

to be my fortune in this life, joined with a strong propensity of
nature, I might perhaps leave something so written to after times
as they should not willingly let it die.

"This one thing I do," has been the path to high usefulness in
life. Even a mediocre nature with a definite aim will accomplish
far more and rise higher than the most talented man in the world
without a goal.

SELFISHNESS

It is important to have a purpose, an ambition, but it is dangerous to let that purpose end with self. The man whose tomb
was never occupied, Absalom, had a definite end in view. He
wanted to be famous in life and remembered in death. But his
ambition ended with himself. The result was a carcass under a
stone pile.

James Barrie tells of how he went in to see the tailor in his town
and spread out before him his set of photographs of the poets, a
symbol of his own ambition. The tailor looked at them silently for
a time, and then turning to the lad quoted to him the line of
Abraham Cowley:

> What can I do to be forever known,
> And make the age to come, my own?[1]

He discovered that the old tailor was thinking of his own young
days when that couplet sang in his head, and he, too, had thirsted to
set off for London in quest of literary fame. But he was afraid; and
while he hesitated, old age came, and found him grasping a box iron.

No young man or young woman should be discouraged from
entertaining the highest ambitions. There is no reason why those
lines should not be echoing in your mind:

> What can I do to be forever known,
> And make the age to come, my own?

There is no reason why some of the most notable places in this

---

1. "The Motto."

nation should not be occupied by young men or young women of high ambition. They should make their aim as high as possible.

> Greatly begin! though thou have time
> But for a line, be that sublime—
> Not failure, but low aim is crime.[2]

Immanuel Kant said, "Always treat a human being as a person, that is, as an end in himself, and not merely as a means to your end." Absalom treated everybody, even his own father, as a means to his end. Men whose ambition ends with themselves often discover that their ambition ends them. As soon as it becomes apparent that what the man aims at is just the glorification and exaltation of himself, the world soon forsakes him. The costly pillar of fame that he has reared stands without a tenant.

It is a curious but interesting and rather striking fact that hardly any of the men who eagerly set out to seek the presidency of the United States were elected to that high office. Men highly qualified and highly gifted, often far abler than men who defeated them, eagerly sought the office, and failed to secure it. Such men were Webster, Clay, Blaine. Most of the men elected president were not men who had spent much of their time or strength seeking the office.

The main ambition we should have is to rear a character which shall be worthy of men's trust and possibly used of God for the good of mankind. The lifting of oneself into any place must be thought of only as an end which is a means to a larger end.

"Utterly selfish" was the comment of a college professor upon one of the eminent men of our day; he was utterly selfish when he knew him as a student. A brilliant minister who in the end made a complete shipwreck of his career, when advised to take a course plainly pointed out by regard for others and by honor and duty, responded that he could not do it; it would "destroy his career." The man was thinking about his career and his success in this world. His career was indeed wrecked; but not in the way in which he had anticipated.

The ends we aim at must be our country's, our fellow men's, our God's, and truth's. With such an aim we cannot be false to

2. James Russell Lowell, "For an Autograph."

ourselves. When one stands by that stone pile in the wood of Ephraim, and then thinks of the marble sarcophagus and mausoleum which Absalom built to perpetuate his name to succeeding generations, there comes to mind the words of our Lord: "Whosoever exalteth himself shall be abased; and he that humbleth himself shall be exalted." Standing by the open grave of John Brown on a mountaintop in the Adirondacks, Wendell Phillips said: "How some men struggle into oblivion, while others forget themselves into immortality!"

IRREVERENCE

In his autobiography of seventy years Senator George F. Hoar paid his respects to one of his colleagues, the brilliant senator from Kansas, John James Ingalls. Ingalls was the author of the best lines ever written on opportunity:

> Master of human destinies am I!
> Fame, love, and fortune on my footsteps wait.
> Cities and fields I walk; I penetrate
> Deserts and seas remote, and passing by
> Hovel and mart and palace, soon or late
> I knock unbidden once at every gate!
> If sleeping, wake—if feasting, rise before
> I turn away. It is the hour of fate,
> And they who follow me reach every state
> Mortals desire, and conquer every foe
> Save death; but those who doubt or hesitate,
> Condemned to failure, penury and woe,
> Seek me in vain and uselessly implore:
> I answer not, and I return no more![3]

Of the author of this poem Senator Hoar said:

John James Ingalls was in many respects one of the brightest intellects I ever knew. One of the few things—I don't know but I might say the only thing—for which he seemed to have any reverence was the character of Mark Hopkins.

---

3. "Opportunity."

When last heard of, this brilliant orator and writer was reporting a prize fight in Nevada. If the end of his life was not in keeping with his ambitions and with his abilities, the secret of the failure must have been that lack of reverence to which Hoar makes reference.

In his *Wilhelm Meister*, Goethe puts into the mouth of one of the characters his own views on education. There he speaks of what are generally referred to as the "three reverences": reverence for what is above; reverence for our equals; reverence for what is beneath us, the poor, the weak, the lowly, the ignorant—the reverence that came into the world through Jesus Christ. We might make another classification also: reverence for self, reverence for others, reverence for God.

A man must revere himself.

> Self-reverence, self-knowledge, self-control,
> These three alone lead life to sovereign power.[4]

John Randolph of Virginia, brilliant but unhappy genius, speaking of ambitions said, "Make to yourself an image, and in defiance of the Decalogue, worship it, whether it be excellence in medicine or law or political eminence; determine not to relax your endeavors until you have attained it." This splendid exhortation to perseverance and determination and self-denial in seeking one's desired goal is altogther praiseworthy and commendable, but for one phrase—"in defiance of the Decalogue" This is precisely the way in which Absalom sought his ambitions—in defiance of the Decalogue. He was ambitious to fill a great place in life and a greater place in death. But he had no reverence for himself. In the Bible, Esau is perhaps the chief example of a man who lost all through the lack of reverence. He is described as that "profane person." Nothing was sacred to him, not even his own birthright. He was not without an appreciation of its value, for he wept over it when he had lost it. But when he came in hungry from the fields and smelled the pottage that his brother was stewing, he put the gratification of that appetite above all else and made the bargain which he was to regret for the rest of his life. So he is handed down to posterity as the man who satisfied a lower appetite at the expense of the higher, a profane—that is, "unfenced"— man in

---

4. Tennyson, "Oenone."

whom there was nothing sacred or temple-like or holy, and who for one morsel of pottage sold his birthright.

When we read of John Milton's ambition, and how he succeeded in writing something which the world has not permitted to die, we must place side by side with this the record of his conduct when a student at Christ College, Cambridge. Because he refused to join the dissipations and revels of the other students, he was known as the "lady of Christ's." But he was willing to endure ridicule and reproach rather than defile the body, which is the temple of the Holy Ghost. In one of the noblest prose passages Milton ever penned he spoke of that "just and pious reverence for my own person." Woe to that man who has no just and pious reverence for his own person!

With reverence for self there must be reverence for others—for their rights, for their feelings, for their sufferings. Intent upon his own desire for a great place, Absalom broke his father's heart, drove him from his capital, and involved the whole nation in the horrors of civil war. What a retribution was meted out to this man who trampled on the rights and feelings of others, and had no respect for anything but his own desires! Instead of sitting on a throne and receiving the plaudits of a loyal and affectionate people, there was Absalom, hanging by his own hair—the emblem of his vanity and overvaulting ambition, all alone in the wood of Ephraim, with none to comfort him or receive from him a farewell message. The loneliest man is not the man who sits in a home out of which has been taken by death the companion of many years; not the man who is a stranger, away from friends and companions and familiar scenes and sights. No! the loneliest person is that person who has been living to himself and therefore has only himself for company. He is like a coffin—room for himself and no one else.

It goes without saying that Absalom lacked the third reverence, reverence for God. Just a small portion of religion might have kept him back from his sin and crime and dismal end. In one of the letters which he wrote to his son, James G. Blaine, who knew what it was to fail in an earthly ambition, said, "There is no success in this life that is not founded on virtue and purity and religious consecration of all we have to God." And so a wiser man wrote to his son long ago, "My son, the fear of the Lord is the beginning of knowledge." Even did this life end all, the man who tries to get along without God is the loser. Godliness is profitable for all things, having the promise of this life as well as of that which is to come. It claims both worlds for its empire and promises its blessings both here and hereafter. No matter how able a man may be, or how far he has risen, if he is a godless man he has missed the great thing for which we have been sent into this world of trial. A look of deepest sadness haunts the brow of the strong, successful man who is a godless man. The higher he has risen, the deeper the sorrow. He possesses everything but the one great thing. He achieves every success but the greatness of faith. "Seek ye first," said Jesus Christ, "the kingdom of God and his righteousness; and all these things shall be added unto you." At first we are inclined to doubt this, but life will show us the truth of it.

We commenced with that beautiful but empty mausoleum and tomb in the king's dale—the tomb of Absalom, the son of David. Let us conclude with another empty tomb, in the garden of Joseph of Arimathaea, the tomb of Jesus, the true Son of David. The first tomb speaks of wrecked ambition, blasted hopes, prostituted powers. The second speaks of a glorious work triumphantly finished. The tomb of Absalom tells of a man who found his life and lost it, who loved himself and exalted himself, with the result that he won a stone pile for a grave and a people's execration. But the tomb in the garden tells of a man who lost his life and found it, who humbled himself and was exalted. Death, unable to hold him, released him and let him go. The tomb of Absalom speaks of the failure and breakdown and disappointment of a life that is not built upon God. The tomb of Jesus speaks of the life that lives forever because it lives unto God.

11

TRUTH BUT NOT THE WHOLE TRUTH—DOEG

"And David said, I knew it that day, when Doeg the Edomite was there, that he would surely tell Saul." (1 Samuel 22:22)

When we come to this man Doeg, we feel like leaving out the "e" and letting it stand as just plain "dog." Among the faces that look down upon us from the Old Testament gallery, there is none more sinister than this face of Doeg. He is a sort of Old Testament Iago.

David had fled from the court of Saul to Nob, where were the tabernacle and the priests. The priest Ahimelech came to meet David trembling, plainly disturbed at David's sudden appearance and at his coming alone. He asked, "Why art thou alone, and no man with thee?"

David then told him a plausible lie, that he was on the king's business, a business so secret that none but himself and Saul might know it. Hence his solitary appearance at the tabernacle.

Satisfied with this explanation, the priest let David eat of the shewbread which had been displayed before the Lord, for it was one of those emergencies when the first duty of religion was humanity. Here, too, David got a weapon, the mighty sword of Goliath with which he had cut off that monster's head in the vale of Elah, and which had been carefully preserved in the tabernacle. As David looked upon the shining blade, revived by the memories of his great feat, he exclaimed, "Give it me; there is none like that!" and he grasped the hilt with his two hands. Thus armed and refreshed, David hastened to leave the place. But as he went out, he saw Doeg, the chief herdsman of Saul, leaning against a pillar; and the moment he saw him, he knew that Doeg purposed evil in his heart. From Nob, David fled to the court of Achish, the king of Gath. Here he escaped detection and arrest by feigning madness and scrabbling on the doors of the gate.

Saul pursued him as far as Gibeah and then, angered at his escape and troubled by an evil spirit, he summoned his advisers and courtiers, and said to them:

> All of you have conspired against me, and there is none that sheweth to me that my son hath made a league with the son of Jesse; and there is none of you that is sorry for me; or sheweth unto me that my son hast stirred up my servant against me, to lie in wait, as at this day.

None of his followers answered him, fearing, perhaps, to anger him further, or secretly hoping that David, general favorite, would make good his escape. But Doeg was on hand. He broke the silence by saying, "I saw the son of Jesse coming to Nob, to Ahimelech the son of Ahitub. And he inquired of the Lord for him, and gave him victuals, and gave him the sword of Goliath, the Philistine."

In a transport of fury, certain now that Ahimelech was a traitor, Saul ordered the aged priest brought before him and thus accused him. "Why have ye conspired against me, thou and the son of Jesse, in that thou hast given him bread, and a sword, and hast enquired of God for him, that he should rise against me, to lie in wait, as at this day?"

Astounded and hurt at the charge of disloyalty, the old priest protested his innocence, saying that he had supposed Saul would be pleased that he had assisted the king's son-in-law in the time of need, for who, he asked, "is so faithful among all thy servants as David? . . . Let not the king impute any thing unto his servant, . . . for thy servant knew nothing of all this, less or more."

His words must have impressed all who heard them with their truthfulness; but Saul was in one of those moments of insane anger when a man neither desires to hear the truth nor is capable of hearing it. "Thou shalt surely die, Ahimelech, thou, and all thy father's house!" he shouted, and called upon his bodyguard to fall upon Ahimelech with their swords. But none of the guard would lift a hand to slay the priest of the Lord. Saul then called on Doeg to perform the cruel and sacrilegious deed. Doeg, nothing loath, drew out his sword and slew Ahimelech and eighty-five priests that day that did wear the linen ephod. One of Ahimelech's sons survived the massacre and fled after David. When David heard the tidings, he said, "I knew it that day, when Doeg the Edomite was there, that he would surely tell Saul: I have occasioned the death of all the persons of thy father's house."

Ahimelech fell a victim to the sword of slander. There Ahimelech lay, the priest of God and all his house with him, slain by the sword of slander—he and many another since. Nevermore will he inquire of God in man's behalf. Nevermore will he offer the atoning sacrifice. Nevermore will he put on the ephod and the breastplate and read the will of God and the destiny of man in the scintillation of the mystic jewels. His priestly race is run; his holy invocations are ended. Not for crimes or sins of his own did he perish, but for a fault put upon him by a lying tongue. His long years of unfaltering loyalty availed him nothing; nothing his guileless tongue and his holy life. Slander marked him for her victim. Had he been as chaste as ice, as pure as snow, yet would he not have escaped the whisperings of the slanderer. His starlike loyalty, his zeal for God's holy house and for his king anointed, only served to make him a shining mark at which the wicked shot his arrows.

THE SLANDERER

Doeg was a past master in the art of defamation of character by slander. The man who goes about loudly proclaiming and denouncing the vices of another man is generally regarded either as a fool or as a man who has an ax to grind. What he says to another's discredit gains little credence. The real and damnable injury is done by an adroit and accomplished liar like Doeg. It was not what he said about Ahimelech that ruined the priest in Saul's regard, but what he insinuated. Everything that Doeg reported was true. David had come to the priest's house. He had been given the shewbread to eat and the sword of Goliath for a weapon; and quite likely the priest had inquired of the Lord for him. All this was true; but it was told in such a way, and told at such a time, as to leave the impression in the mind of Saul that Ahimelech was in conspiracy against him. When a witness takes the stand in court, he is adjured to tell not only the truth but the whole truth. Doeg told the truth but not the whole truth. He didn't tell that David had deceived Ahimelech as to the reason for his coming, saying that he was on secret business for the king. With this important fact omitted, and the rest of the meeting told with an accent of innuendo, the suspicion of Saul was aroused; and the innocent priest, thus slandered, went to his doom.

Sometimes slander is born of revenge, as when Joseph was slandered in the house of Potiphar. Sometimes it comes out of pride and hate, and the innate selfishness of human nature; and sometimes it appears as a dreadful trait without any reason save the depravity of human nature. There are those who prey upon the reputation of others, not for the sake of any real or imagined benefit they derive from it, but solely out of the delight of a fallen nature in the laceration of character and the massacre of reputation.

The strange thing is that the most ignorant knave or fool can get a hearing. If he offered his opinion on any matter of business or religion or politics or science, he would be laughed at and scorned. But let him take up an evil reproach against his neighbor, and he gets just as silent and respectful a hearing as if he were a man of great discretion and judgment. The slanderer's trade is the meanest because it takes away that which is precious. Even a bad man has something good about him, and the less he has of it the more precious it becomes. This sin is the meanest because it is the most cowardly too. It is not an open assault but a blow in the dark, an arrow shot under cover. David described this sort of man well when he said, "The wicked bend their bow, they make ready their arrow upon the string, that they may privily shoot at the upright in heart." The slanderer is like those mountaineers who lie down behind a log and, safe in concealment, aim their rifle at the heart of the unsuspecting mountaineer on another path. The slanderer is the submarine of human society, prowling submerged in darkness and discharging his missile at those who go up and down the paths of life on the errands of peace and good will. Here human nature touches bottom, if, indeed, it has a bottom. The slanderer slights the worthiest in the land,

> Sneers at the just; contemns the brave,
> And blackens goodness in its grave.[1]

No weed grows so quickly as defamation and slander. It spreads like a miasma. Take a bottle of ink, upset it on a white blotter, and watch how the black stain spreads quickly across the white. So the ink of slander covers with Stygian blackness the fair surface of a good name.

Nothing is easier than to take an incident or event, in itself perfectly innocent, and give it an evil color and interpretation. This was the case with Doeg and the aged priest. Just a little left out, and emphasis misplaced, and the innocent priest was painted as a traitor and conspirator. There is a curious example of this in the life of Lincoln, who, with nearly all our public men, was a mark for the arrow of slander and detraction. It is one of the sad traits of human nature to think evil of those who have risen a few degrees above us. One of the perils of democracy, undoubtedly, is the reluctance of men of ability to stand for public office, because they do not wish to subject themselves and their families to the almost inevitable torrent of abuse, misrepresentation, and slander. After the battle of Antietam, Lincoln went down to visit Mc Clellan and the army, remaining for four days and then returning to Washington. Soon an ugly undercurrent of rumor was flowing to the effect that Lincoln, driving over the battlefield, had asked for a comic and indecent song to be sung.

In the political campaign of 1864 this was openly asserted. One of the chief papers of New York asserted that a day or two after the battle, Lincoln was driving over the field with McClellan, his bodyguard, Colonel Lamon, and some other officers. When they came to the stone bridge, Burnside's Bridge, where the dead lay in heaps, Lincoln, slapping the thigh of Lamon, exclaimed, "Lamon, give us that song about the 'Picayune Butler.' General McClellan has never heard it."

Whereupon McClellan raised his hand in deprecation and said, "No, Mr. President, not now; anything but that here."

---

1. William Watson, "The Woman with the Serpent's Tongue."

With this for a start one of the campaign songs for 1864 was as follows:

> Abe may crack his jolly jokes,
> O'er bloody fields of stricken battle,
> While yet the ebbing life tide smokes,
> From men that die like butchered cattle.
> He, ere yet the guns grow cold,
> To pimps and pets may crack his stories.

Lincoln was greatly pained and distressed at the slander, and took the trouble to write a long account of what actually happened on the visit. This was to go as a letter from Colonel Lamon to one who had inquired as to the truth of the slander. However, Lincoln determined at the last to make no reply. But the letter tells what actually took place.

On the visit to Antietam the President, riding in an ambulance with McClellan and other officers, not a day or two after the battle but two weeks after the battle, and where there was not a grave that had not been rained on since it was dug, in one of his melancholy moods asked Lamon to sing a little ballad called "Forty Years Ago"—the singing of which Lamon said had often brought tears to Lincoln's eyes as he had listened to it on the circuit in Illinois or at the White House. The song commences,

> I've wandered to the village, Tom,
> I've sat beneath the tree.

The ballad then goes on to relate the feelings of a man who returned to his native village after an absence of forty years and found everything changed and all his friends gone. This was the song for which Lincoln had asked. But at the conclusion of it, in order to lift him out of his melancholy, Lamon, at his own initiative, did sing the comic but altogether harmless song, "The Picayune Butler." These were the facts. Yet thousands believed that Abraham Lincoln was the sort of man who would call for a comic and indecent song when driving past the bodies of the men who had fallen in battle for the maintenance of the Union.

THE SLANDERER'S HELPERS

We all despise the deliberate liar and slanderer; yet how true it is that he would make no headway in his despicable business were it not for the assistance which he gets from others. One launches and sets afloat an evil report, but generally others carelessly and thoughtlessly carry it down the stream of human life. How often most of us, perhaps all of us, have been guilty of spreading a rumor. So men say, "Did you hear?" "Can it be true?" "I don't believe it, but—" and thus the rumor is blown. The psalmist's description of the good man is a man who not only refrains from lying about his neighbor, but will not even take up an evil reproach against him. Unfortunately, in the present dislocation and fallen state of human nature, there is that which makes men take a degree of delight in hearing evil of another.

Slander is an injury which it is hard to undo, even when one might desire to do so. A peasant had slandered a friend, only to find out later that what he had said was not true. Troubled in his conscience he went to a monk to seek advice.

The monk said to him, "If you want to make peace with your conscience, you must fill a bag with feathers and go to every dooryard in the village and drop in each of them one feather."

The peasant did as he was told and, returning to the monk, announced that he done penance for his sin.

"Not yet!" said the monk sternly. "Take up your bag, go the rounds again, and gather up every feather that you have dropped."

"But," exclaimed the peasant, "the wind has blown them all away by this time!"

"Yes, my son," answered the monk, "and so it is with gossip and slander. Words are easily dropped, but no matter how hard you try you never can get them back again."

If the Old Testament portrait of the noble man is that of a man who will not take up an evil reproach against his neighbor, it certainly is the portrait of the noble New Testament man, where Peter speaks of that love which "covers a multitude of sins"; and where in his matchless lyric of Christian love Paul speaks of the love that "thinketh no evil" and "rejoiceth not in iniquity." An evil reproach should be spoken only when it is true, and then only when the speaking of it is necessary for the safeguarding of honor and virtue. Never otherwise! Fathers and mothers may sometimes think that even their best efforts and example have little effect upon their children. But they should not be deceived or discouraged. Something that they have done or said will be ever before their child when they have long been in their graves. My father has been in his grave for forty years, but there is one thing, among many other splendid things, which I remember concerning him, and that is that only once did I hear him speak ill of another, and that was when it was necessary in order to warn and guard his children.

The cure for defamation, gossip, and slander is a converted soul and the love of Christ in our hearts. Then, instead of delighting in dragging out, exposing, and exaggerating the faults of others, we shall do what we can to cover them with the mantle of charity.

> Teach me to feel another's woe,
> To hide the fault I see;
> The mercy I to others show,
> That mercy show to me.[2]

---

2. Pope, "Universal Prayer."

12

SACKCLOTH WITHIN—JEHORAM

"And, behold, he had sackcloth within upon his flesh." (2 Kings 6:30)

O n the road from Nazareth to Jerusalem, after crossing the plain of Esdraelon and the field of Dothan, we pass a bald and lofty mountain crowned with a miserable Arab village, around which are the gray and yellow ruins of the walls and streets of an ancient city. It is all that is left of Samaria, the capital of the northern kingdom of Israel and the city which was founded by Omri. Climbing the winding road to the summit of the hill, we think of Samaria as it was in the day of its power and splendor. There we overtake grim Elijah on his way to rebuke wicked Ahab and savage Jezebel. There too we overtake Elisha leading up to Samaria the blinded Syrian soldiers who had been sent to seize him at Dothan. As we go up the winding road, we meet Naaman in a rage, lashing his horses and driving furiously down the mountain, because, after he had come all the way from Damascus to Samaria to be healed of his leprosy. Elisha had not even gone out to talk with him but had sent his servant to tell him to go and wash seven times in the river Jordan.

As we approach the ruins of the city, we remember the terrible siege of Samaria by the Syrian army; and how finally the Syrians, having heard a false rumor that the king of Israel had hired the dreaded Hittites to fight for him, evacuated their camps and fled in terror homeward. The news of this was brought to the city by four lepers who wandered into the Syrian camp and found it deserted.

While the siege of Samaria was at it worst, however, Samaria was tightly shut up. The famine in the city was so great, and the hunger so bitter, that the head of an unclean and forbidden beast, the ass, was sold for eighty pieces of silver.

In order to encourage the people of the city to endure hardship and resist the Syrian foe, Jehoram walked along the walls of the city. As he made his rounds, he was accosted by a woman who cried to him, "Help, my lord, O king!" At the king's request she made known her desire. She had made a bargain with another woman that they should eat their sons on succeeding days. She had kept her part of the bargain, and with the other mother had killed and eaten her own child. But now that the pangs of hunger were appeased, maternity had reasserted itself in the second mother and she had hidden her son.

"Can a mother forget her sucking child, that she should not have compassion on the son of her womb?" is the question in Isaiah. Were it not for the plain record of history, we should be inclined to say, No; a mother cannot forget her child, still less practice the horrible act related here.

We could hardly give credence to this story except that the same thing has often happened, notably at the siege of Jerusalem. Jeremiah had prophesied that the people of Jerusalem would eat their own sons and daughters; and that was what actually happened.

There is no tyranny like the tyranny of hunger and the dominion of the flesh. At the time of the gold rush to California, the Donner party, made up of high-class religious people from Illinois and other Midwest states, was overtaken by the snows in the Sierras at what is now Donner Lake, where most of them perished. It is a matter of record that the stronger waited eagerly for the weaker to die that they might devour their bodies. Even murder was committed so the survivors could devour the corpse.

A survivor of Andersonville, the Confederate prison in Georgia, related how hunger gradually stripped from the starving prisoners the principles of honor and chivalry and humanity which obtain under ordinary circumstances. He related that two men who had been bosom friends and comrades during the war, and also within the terrible prison stockade, lay side by side, growing weaker and weaker. Each was eagerly waiting for the other to die so that he might seize his handful of beans and bread. Impatient, the one whose strength was greater choked his comrade to death—only to expire himself in a few minutes.

Amazed and horrified at what the Samaritan woman had told him, the king Jehoram rent his clothes, as people did in that day under the stress of great emotion. As he did so, those who stood about were surprised to see that the king had sackcloth within. Until that moment the garments which they had seen were the garments of a monarch, wrought of purple and fine linen; but now they saw upon the king's flesh the coarse brown rags of sackcloth!

INVISIBLE BURDENS

Sackcloth under fine garments reminds us that invisible burdens of care, distress, anxiety, and sorrow are often carried by those who, to an outside view, are without them. The recollection of this is of a nature to deliver us from envy and discontent.

In distributing her garments life gives a few yards of sackcloth to every person. Who would have thought that this king of Israel, walking so bravely and defiantly along the beleaguered walls with his fine garments flashing in the sunlight, had sackcloth on his flesh? We draw water, each with his own cup, and each cup is chased with a different design; but we all drink out of the same well. John Morley in the story of his life speaks of how he had met "the usual joys and sorrows of life." It is well to remember that there are joys and there are sorrows which are "usual," especially when we are tempted to feel that our sorrow or difficulty is unusual.

> If every man's internal care
> Were written on his brow,
> How many would our pity share,
> Who have our envy now![1]

The tenth commandment is probably the one which is most frequently and generally broken by men, and the penalties for its breaking are the least feared. Yet it was not put in the Decalogue without good reason, and its penalties are bitter and disastrous. Envy, like the sun, beats with its scorching rays on everything that

---

1. Pietro Metastatio, "Giuseppe Riconosciuto."

is high and great and different. Envy, like Haman, hangs itself on the gallows which it erects for others.

The famous, the great, the notable, the learned, the rich, are very commonly the object of envy. But that is because men do not see the sackcloth which these persons wear upon their flesh beneath the outer garments of their fame, or wealth, or station. One of the best cures for envy would be to watch closely the persons who are the objects of envy, and see, when some wind of life blows the outer garments aside, that there is sackcloth within. It would let us know that godliness with contentment is great gain, and would move us to repeat the prayer of Agur, "Give me neither poverty nor riches; feed me with food convenient for me: lest I be full and deny thee, and say, Who is the Lord? or lest I be poor, and steal, and take the name of my God in vain."

SACKCLOTH AND SYMPATHY

The remembrance that sackcloth often hides beneath brave and fine outer garments, and that secret and hidden burdens are carried by all men, not only delivers us from envy, but moves us to sympathy and compassion. It takes the edge off the tongue of our bitter criticism and cures the anger or malice of the heart. When you raise aloft the harpoon of your quick, rash, and bitter judgment to sink it in a brother's body, pause for a moment to reflect that there is much in him that you cannot know and see. For that very weakness or sin for which you judge him he may often be on his knees in bitter remorse or desperate struggle. That which has been done wrongly you can compute, but know not what has been resisted. Where you least expect it there may be the sackcloth of some secret and inner grief, struggle, or difficulty—a physical malady or thorn in the flesh, a battle with temptation, an ever-present sorrow, an ever-gnawing anxiety.

There is another invisible burden which men often bear, and that is the burden of some sin that has been committed, a sin of which the world at large knows nothing. But the scar and the burden of the transgression are there, and the man who bears this burden can say with the psalmist, "My sin is ever before me." If we could lift the veil which hides one life from another, how many burdens of secret sin we would see—the heaviest burden of all.

Thus envy and covetousness, vindictive and bitter criticism, are mortally wounded when men get a glimpse of the sackcloth within. In one of his letters David Livingstone gives eloquent expression to this truth that the purple may very often cover sackcloth. He had come back to England from Africa to be decked with honors and greeted as a hero. But he had a wayward son Robert who at that time was fighting in the Union Army. To his friend Livingstone writes: "I hope your son will do well in the distant land to which he has gone. My son is in the Federal Army in America, and no comfort. The secret ballast is often applied by a kind hand above, when to outsiders we appear to be sailing gloriously with the wind."

Let us go softly then, speak gently, deal kindly with all, for those who wear sackcloth are everywhere near us.

> If we knew the cares and trials
> Knew the effort all in vain,
> And the bitter disappointment,
> Understood the loss and gain,
> Would the grim, eternal roughness
> Seem, I wonder, just the same?
> Should we help where now we hinder,
> Should we pity where we blame?
>
> Could we but draw back the curtains
> That surround each other's lives,
> See the naked heart and spirit,
> Know what spur the action gives,
> Often we should find it better,
> Purer than we judged we should;
> We should love each other better
> If we only understood.[2]

Recently a secretary of the American Bible Society was traveling from New York to Pittsburgh. In the dining car he sat down with three other men who were strangers to him. After a little he asked the waiter, who seemed to be new and nervous on the job, for a glass of water. After a time when it was not brought to him, he asked again.

---

2. Author unknown.

One of the other men at the table said, "Let's each put fifty cents into a pool and make a guess as to the number of times we ask before we get a glass of water."

The secretary replied, "I am a minister, opposed to gambling, and will not bet." He asked for the water seven times before the waiter brought it. Later, just as the four men were about to leave the table, the waiter came up to them and apologized for his poor service. The secretary said to him, "I suppose a new man does have a time getting used to serving on a moving train."

But the waiter answered, "I am not a new man. I have been doing this work for years; but just before the train left New York, I received a telephone call telling me that our fourteen-year-old daughter had just been killed by an auto." He had continued the trip because two other waiters had failed to report for duty, and the officials promised to send him back "deadhead" on the first train leaving Pittsburgh after his arrival. The secretary and the other three men who had been impatient and annoyed at the poor service the waiter had given them were much chagrined and humbled. Sackcloth within!

SECRET REPENTANCE

The hidden sackcloth is a figure for that repentance and humiliation which men may experience and yet hide from the world. When Jehoram rent his clothes, disclosing the sackcloth, the sackcloth revealed that there was in him at least some slight acknowledgment of God, some slight humiliation before him. It was a halfway confession that the famine and suffering of the siege were a judgment from God, and at least an inclination or movement in the direction of repentance. Yet the king had been careful to hide all this from the public; he wore the sackcloth but hid it under his robes of royalty.

There are more men like that walking along the walls of life than we imagine. When we talk of a hypocrite, we mean the man who pretends to be better than he really is. Perhaps in a day when church membership was a *sine qua non* and the man who did not go to church was looked upon as a social outcast, there was a stronger temptation to wear the garment of a formal religion without any purpose of performing the duties of religion than there is today. But there is another kind of hypocrisy: not the man who pretends to be better than he is, but the man who pretends to be worse than he is. Before the people Jehoram pretended to be without any anxiety, or any humiliation, or any feeling of repentance, while all the time that was in his heart.

The average man has a tendency to hide and disguise whatever religion or spirituality he has. Men have a repentance and a faith which they often hide from the world. Underneath a brave, defiant, worldly, and irreligious front there may be found secret regret for what they are not, a secret sigh for something better, a hidden struggle against temptation, a regard for the Word of God, and perhaps an occasional but sincere prayer. Yet all this is carefully hidden from the world. One would never know it was there.

The biography of a former United States senator is a book which will bring sadness, and ought to bring alarm, to all those who have the welfare of their country at heart, for in the portrait of this man we find unreserved and undisguised scorn for public and even personal morality. Nothing could be more sordid than what is related in the pages of this book. Yet at the end of the book there is just a flash of light which discloses another man than the man of Gargantuan appetite and cynical disregard for public and private morality. When he was stricken with his last sickness and was being wheeled about in a chair, his once-gigantic frame now shrunken and haggard, this senator said to his faithful valet, "William, I want you to tell me the truth, not what the doctors tell me, but the truth. Do you think I'm getting better?"

Tearfully the said, "Senator, I will tell you the truth. You are not far from the end. Amen."

At that the senator lifted a once-mighty hand and said, "Then, William, when you go to church tomorrow, put up a prayer for me." "And, behold, he had sackcloth within!"

The noblest thing in your heart is its thought of God, its sorrow for sin, its hope of eternal life. If you have that in your heart, then give full expression to it. Do not hide the sackcloth with the outer garments. Do not wait for an expression and confession of the faith that is in you until it is too late to bless your life here, or to make it a blessing to others. All faith, repentance, and religious desire come out to a climax in the complete humbling of oneself before the Son of God. There no hidden confession will suffice, for Jesus said, "Whosoever therefore shall confess me before men, him will I confess." When a man makes that confession and comes before God in true humility and repentance, then he is clothed, not with the rags of his own self-righteousness, but with that robe which has been washed so white by the crimson tide that flows for sinners at the foot of the Cross.

13

MAN AGAINST GOD—PHARAOH

"And Pharaoh said, Who is the Lord, that I should obey his voice, to let Israel go?" (Exodus 5:2)

W ho is the Lord?" Pharaoh was soon to learn who the Lord is! Pharaoh is one of the major characters of the Bible. Dramatic and stirring incidents in the history of Israel and the history of revelation and redemption are associated with his name. This is the fullest account that we have of a duel between God and man, between the power of this world and the power of God. It is also a true picture of the unregenerate heart in rebellion against God.

Somewhere near Thebes, or Memphis, or perhaps near the site of the present Cairo where the Great Pyramid rears itself above the desert, stood the palace of Pharaoh. The ruins which have been unearthed give us some conception of Egyptian buildings, imperial palaces, colossal tombs and temples.

On this day so memorable in the history of mankind Moses and his brother Aaron walked in cloudless sunshine down the long avenue flanked with sphinxes which, with stony, unchanging, impassive look, gazed off into space—into the past ages and into the ages to come—as if they were the incarnation of the mystery of time and history. At the end of the avenue stood the palace of Pharaoh. In front was a huge wall rising above massive columns, and in the wall a gateway. Through this gateway Moses and Aaron passed into the hall of Pharaoh, the Child of the Sun. In front of the walls, on either side of the palace, stood double rows of red sandstone columns. Some of them were wound about with serpents and crowned with fierce birds, in whose eyes and talons flashed and gleamed precious stones. Here a stately pillar blossomed into flowers at the top, and yonder a fountain climbed "the ladder of the sun."

Along the two sides of the palace enclosure soldiers of Egypt stood at rigid attention. On the gilded and enameled throne sat Pharaoh, the lord of the whole earth. In front, and on either side of him, stood armed guards; and slaves with enormous fans decorated with jewels stirred a breath of coolness for the Child of the Sun. On the wall behind the throne were sculptures and reliefs in red and blue, the colors in which the Egyptians delighted. Some of them, depicted the victories and conquests of the Pharaohs, and some of them showed the journey of the soul into the land of silence and death. On the head of Pharaoh was the double golden crown, and in his hand the scepter of world dominion.

Moses was quite familiar with this palace, for it was there that he had been brought up as a child when he was taken out of the river Nile by the daughter of Pharaoh—not this Pharaoh, but his predecessor, Pharaoh of the Oppression.

It was here in this palace that Moses made his tremendous decision and took his glorious stand when he "refused to be called the son of Pharaoh's daughter, choosing rather to suffer affliction with the people of God than to enjoy the pleasures of sin for a season; esteeming the reproach of Christ greater riches than the treasures in Egypt." As we behold Pharaoh on his throne and the splendor and glory of his palace, with one of the great pyramids rising towards the blue sky in the distance, we begin to have some idea of how great and rich the treasures of Egypt were. It was forty years, however, since Moses had been there. During these forty years he had been a shepherd in the wilderness in the land of Midian. Now he has come back to the scenes of his youth. Perhaps he recognized some of his boyhood companions among the officers and guards of Pharaoh's household. But none of them recognized in this son of the desert, bronzed by forty years of life in Midian, the friend of their youth.

Speaking in the Egyptian tongue which he knew so well Moses said to Pharaoh, "Thus saith the Lord God of Israel, Let my people go."

That was something new and strange for the Child of the Sun

to hear. He was the man who gave orders to the world and received none. But now this bronzed son of the desert, speaking in the name of his God, tells Pharaoh to let Israel go. Pharaoh was quick with his angry and contemptuous answer, "Who is the Lord, that I should obey his voice to let Israel go? I know not the Lord, neither will I let Israel go." This he followed up by telling Aaron and Moses to go back to their labors among the Hebrews. He also gave the order for a new oppression. Henceforth the taskmasters, or slave drivers, must compel the people to make bricks without straw. Because of this new oppression the Hebrews charged Moses with making their lot in Egypt all the more difficult by his demand upon Pharaoh that he let the people go. But the Lord encouraged Moses and said to him, "Now shalt thou see what I will do to Pharaoh." Now begins the great duel between Pharaoh and God.

Meeting Pharaoh on the banks of the Nile, Moses again demanded that he let the people go. When he refused, Moses stretched out his wonder-working rod, and all rivers and fountains of Egypt were turned into blood. The fish in the Nile died, and the river stank. Then the second plague, the plague of the loathsome frogs which swarmed into the houses and bedchambers of the people. Then the third plague came, the plague of lice. After the lice came the flies, still a plague in Egypt as the traveler well knows. And after the flies the pestilence that slew the cattle in the fields; and after that pestilence the plague of boils; and after the boils the plague of thunder and hail. When each of these plagues smote the land, Pharaoh sent for Moses and asked him to entreat the Lord to lift the plague. But each time, after this was done, Pharaoh broke his promise, hardened his heart, and would not let the people go.

After the seventh plague, the plague of thunder and lightning and hail which had stripped the trees and vines and laid low the grain in the fields, Pharaoh sent for Moses and said to him, "I have sinned. . . . The Lord is righteous, and I and my people are wicked." He entreated Moses to ask God to stay the plague. But when this was done, he again hardened his heart. Then came the swarm of the locusts. After this eighth plague Pharaoh sent for Moses and said, as if he really meant it, "I have sinned against the Lord your God, and against you. Now, therefore, forgive, I pray thee, my sin only this once." Again Moses entreated the Lord for him, and a great wind out of the west swept the locusts away and cast them into the Red Sea. But as soon as the locusts were gone, the repentance of Pharaoh was gone. Once more he hardened his heart and refused to let the people go.

Then came the ninth plague, next to the final plague, the most dreadful of all. Moses stretched forth his hand toward heaven, and there was a thick darkness over all the land of Egypt for three days, a darkness that could be felt. In that land where the sun shines more brightly than elsewhere in the world, and where the people are accustomed to the bluest of skies, there was nothing now but darkness. One moment there was light and laughter and song. The merchants were crying their wares; the laborers were tilling their fields; the priests in the temples of Isis and Osiris were worshiping and sacrificing to their gods. The builders were busy with hammer and ax; the royal court was gay with revel and dissipation and the dispatch of great business; the peasant sunned himself by the door of his hut. All the pursuits and engagements of life were in full tide when suddenly the cloud of darkness came down, and laughter was turned into mourning. The song and jest and prayer and curse perished on the lips of those who uttered them. The tools of industry, the instruments of music, and the weapons of war were dropped by nerveless hands. The temples were silent, the tents were still. Where the people stood when the darkness came down, there they sat down for three days and three nights. None rose up from his place, and none saw the face of him who sat next to him. Egypt was dark and silent, for God had blotted out the light of the sun.

In the midst of this dreadful darkness Pharaoh again sent for Moses. This time he told him that he could take the people—the men, the women, and the children—and leave Egypt, but that the flocks and herds were to be left behind. The courageous and uncompromising Moses answered that if they left Egypt, they would not leave "a hoof " behind them.

This enraged Pharaoh, and he drove Moses from his presence, saying to him, "Get thee from me, take heed to thyself, see my face no more; for in that day thou seest my face thou shalt die!" That was the last spoken defiance of Pharaoh. His cup of iniquity was now full.

Moses said to him, "Thou hast spoken well, I will see thy face no more." They did, however, meet again, after the terrible tenth and last plague. But that time Pharaoh urged Moses, with his people and flocks, to leave.

Pharaoh had received warning when the nine previous plagues fell upon him in Egypt. But this time the plague came without warning, for the Lord had hardened the heart of Pharaoh. At the hour of midnight there suddenly arose over all Egypt a great cry, a long wail of woe, a tidal wave of lamentation sweeping over the land. In his marble palace Pharaoh awoke with a sense of dread and called for his first-born son and heir, only to learn that the prince of the realm was dead. Mothers awoke in terror to discover that the babes they clasped to their breasts were silent corpses. In the dungeon the prisoner shook his chain and turned over to find that the prisoner at his side, a first-born son, was dead. In the temples of Isis and Osiris the priests called in vain upon their gods to restore the dead offspring. In the fields even the cattle moaned over their dead, for in that night the angel of the Lord smote the first-born of Egypt, "from the first-born of Pharaoh that sat on his throne unto the first-born of the captive that was in the dungeon; and all the first-born of the cattle." Death reigned! Death in the palace; death in the cottage; death in the temple; death in the dungeon; death in the bazaar; death on the river; death on the highway; death in the fields; death in the desert! Death! Death! Death! Everywhere a cry of anguish went up to Egypt's skies. But in Israel the angel of death passed over the homes where the blood of the lamb was sprinkled; and at midnight Moses led the people forth, for Pharaoh, brought to his knees by this last blow, consented to their departure. In a single night the chains of four hundred years of bondage were struck from Israel. The march of deliverance, the march of the Exodus, had commenced!

When the first wave of anguish had subsided in Egypt, Pharaoh was himself again—the same proud, haughty, defiant, unrepenting soul. Summoning his captains, he put his army on the march to pursue the children of Israel, and overtook them on the shores of the Red Sea. When the people heard the rumble of those six hundred chariots, the neighing of the war horses, and the shouting of the captains, they were sore afraid. They cried out in their fear and reproached Moses, asking him if it was because there were no graves in Egypt that he had brought them out there into the wilderness to die. But Moses, encouraged by God, said to the people, "Fear ye not, stand still, and see the salvation of the Lord, which he will shew to you to day: for the Egyptians whom ye have seen to day, ye shall see them again no more for ever."

When Moses stretched out his rod over the sea, the waters were divided, and a pathway was left for Israel, with the waters a wall unto them on their right hand and on their left; and all the people passed over in safety. But when the Egyptians went down after them in pursuit, "the Lord looked unto the host of the Egyptians through the pillar of fire and of the cloud, and troubled the host of the Egyptians." When Moses again stretched out his hand over the sea, the sea returned and covered the chariots and the horsemen of Pharaoh. When morning dawned, Israel "saw the Egyptians dead upon the sea shore."

So ended the great duel between the lord of this world and the Lord of heaven and earth. As always, God won the battle.

THE WILL OF GOD FOR MAN AND THE WORLD

The extraordinary history of Pharaoh tells us, first of all, that no earthly power can frustrate the will of God. Pharaoh was more than mere man. He was the incarnation of world power, the lord of the whole earth. But when he defied God, he perished. It has ever been so. The father of this pharaoh, the Pharaoh of the Oppression, sought to frustrate the purpose of God in Israel by slaying the male children. But God put his fear in the hearts of the midwives, and they saved the children alive. Then Pharaoh decreed that all male children of the Hebrews should be drowned in the river Nile at their birth. But God put the love of a helpless child in the heart of Pharaoh's own daughter, and Moses was saved alive, the very same Moses who later defied the Pharaoh of the Exodus.

Sennacherib of Assyria and Nebuchadnezzar of Babylon sought to destroy Israel, but they themselves were overthrown and destroyed.

Haman, the prime minister of Persia, persuaded Ahasuerus to issue the infamous decree for the slaughter of all the Jews throughout the Persian empire. But God gave the king a sleepless night, and through that sleepless night he learned of the faithfulness of Mordecai, and through Esther he learned of the wickedness of

Haman. Haman was hanged on the gallows he had built for Mordecai, and Israel was spared.

When Jesus was born at Bethlehem of Judea, Herod the Great—great in his buildings, great in his transgressions and murders—disturbed by the rumors of this new king who was to be born, gave orders for the destruction of all infants two years old and under. But Joseph, warned by the angel of the Lord, took the child into Egypt—the same Egypt which once tried to destroy Israel, now a refuge for the holy family. At length "Herod was dead," and the angel of the Lord said to Joseph, "Arise, and take the young child and his mother, and go into the land of Israel: for they are dead which sought the young child's life."

So it has ever been. Pharaoh perished in the Red Sea; Haman was hanged on the gallows of Mordecai; Herod died in his palace. But the child Jesus lives on forever.

INSINCERE REPENTANCE

Several times it seemed that Pharaoh's heart was softened, and that he was about to turn to God. On two occasions he sent for Moses when the plagues were on him, and said, "I have sinned. Forgive, I pray thee, my sin only this once." He implied that if God lifted the present judgment that was upon him, he would change his ways, and there would be no need ever to impose another infliction. Yet each time when the plague was lifted and the sky was again clear, he went back to his sin.

In this respect Pharaoh has numerous companions in the Bible and thousands upon thousands of companions out of the Bible. Balaam, the eloquent seer of Mesopotamia, was a man who said, "I have sinned," but who really did not mean it. When he was first asked by the king of Moab to come and curse the children of Israel who were marching upon his kingdom, Balaam inquired of the Lord and was told not to go. When the king of Moab sent a second embassy, believing that every man has his price, Balaam haughtily told the ambassadors that if the king of Moab were to give him gold and treasure which would fill his house, he would not go to Moab and curse Israel against the word of the Lord. Yet at the same time he invited the messengers to stay with him another night. That night he thought he got the permission of

God to go, and he saddled his ass and eagerly set out for Moab, intent upon receiving the gold that the king of that land had promised him. On the way he was stopped by an angel with a drawn sword. When he saw the angel, he cried out, "I have sinned; . . . now therefore, if it displease thee, I will get me back again." Yet still his heart was intent upon the bribe that the king of Moab had offered him if he would curse Israel. So eager indeed was he for this gold that even after his eyes had been opened to the glorious destiny of Israel and he had pronounced a marvelous blessing upon Israel, his heart still hankered after Balak's gold. In the end, by a shameful artifice, corrupting the morals of Israel, he received his reward, but also his reward from God, for he was slain in battle with Israel. After we have heard him say, "Let me die the death of the righteous, and let my last end be like his!" it is a shock to find Balaam lying among the heaps of the dead Midianites who fell in battle against Israel. His repentance was only a halfway repentance.

Saul is another man of insincere repentance. More often than any other man in the Bible, Saul said, "I have sinned," and said it with tears, beseeching Samuel to pray for him. Each time it seems that surely Saul has repented; but just a turn of the page reveals the same old Saul again. He hardened his heart so many times that at length the day came when he called upon God in vain, for the Lord answered him not, "neither by dreams, nor by Urim, nor by prophets."

These three men—Pharaoh, Balaam, and Saul—all said, "I have sinned," but said it only to escape from present or impending judgment. As soon as the judgment was over they hardened their hearts and went back to their transgressions.

This is true not only of men like these notable characters of the Bible, but of men in general. It is easy to repent, or to seem to repent, when the way is difficult and hard. But when the way becomes easy again and the storm has subsided, we often go back to our transgressions and follies. After his first experience of a storm at sea Robinson Crusoe vowed that he would never go to sea again:

> In this agony of mind I made many vows and resolutions that if it would please God and spare my life here this one voyage, if ever

> I got once my foot on dry land again, I would go directly home to
> my father and never set it into a ship again as long as I lived.

These feelings lasted while the storm lasted.

> But as the sea was returned to its smoothness of surface by the
> abatement of that storm, so the fury of my thoughts being over,
> my fears and apprehensions of being swallowed up by the sea
> being forgotten, and the current of my former desires returned, I
> entirely forgot the vows and promises that I had made in my
> distress.

Instead of going home to his father and mother, he set out
upon another voyage, "not ashamed to sin, and yet ashamed to
repent."

Beware of halfway repentance, and of repentance that is soon
forgotten.

How Men Harden Their Hearts

Several times in the narrative of this duel between Pharaoh and
God we read that the Lord hardened Pharaoh's heart. This repeated utterance has caused no little scoffing and mocking. "What
kind of a God is this?" unbelievers have asked. "A God who
commands a man to do a thing, then hardens his heart so that he
will not do it, and then punishes him for his disobedience?" The
answer to this objection is found in the record, repeated several
times, that "Pharaoh hardened his heart." There is no conflict in
these two statements, that God hardened Pharaoh's heart and that
Pharaoh hardened his own heart. They are two different ways of
saying the same thing. Yet in the end, and in the beginning, it was
Pharaoh who hardened his heart. It was Pharaoh who said, "Who
is the Lord, that I should obey his voice"; Pharaoh who, as soon as
he was granted respite from the different plagues, again refused to
let the people go; Pharaoh who drove Moses out of his court and
threatened to kill him; Pharaoh who, after the tenth plague and the
death of the first-born, told Moses to take the people and go, but
who quickly changed his mind and pursued them with his army.

Yet it is true, in a certain sense, that the Lord "hardened

Pharaoh's heart." This means that God is the author of the moral laws which sweep through the world, faithful as the stars in their courses, irresistible as gravitation, and universal as God. These moral laws work in the souls of men. One of them is that when a man willfully and knowingly disobeys God, a process of hardening commences. With Pharaoh one disobedience led to another. He resisted both mercy and judgment, and hardened his heart. The metaphor is a sound metaphor. The heart becomes hardened in that it becomes insensitive to the Word of the Spirit. Rain softens the earth; then the sun comes out and bakes it. So it was with Pharaoh. Judgment for a moment softened his heart; but when the plague was lifted, he hardened his heart and returned to his transgression.

In this respect Pharaoh is no solitary monster of iniquity, dealt with by God as God dealt with no other man. No! He did exactly what thousands of persons who resist the Spirit of God and harden their hearts are doing today.

How merciful, long-suffering, and patient God is! His dealings with Pharaoh show that. He might have wiped out Pharaoh in a moment! Instead of that he let him repeatedly challenge him and defy him. Again and again he sent Moses to tell Pharaoh to let the people go. He visited him with every kind of judgment and affliction, from flies to the terrible death of the first-born; and every time Pharaoh turned toward God and said he would obey him, the judgment was lifted; but every time Pharaoh went back to his sinful way. Pharaoh resisted both mercy and judgment until at length his hour had passed, and in defiance to God he perished in the waters of the Red Sea.

God speaks to you and me as plainly as he did to Pharaoh. He speaks to us with his mercies and with his judgments. He weaves the web of our lives with both mercy and judgment. Therefore beware of hardening your heart against God, for there can come a time when that hard heart of resistance to God's Holy Spirit becomes the final state.

One of the most learned professors who ever occupied a chair at Princeton Theological Seminary was Joseph Addison Alexander, a professor in the seminary from 1830 until his death in 1860. His scholarly attainments are almost unbelievable. He was the master of seven languages, could read and write fourteen more, and had a reading knowledge of five others—twenty-six in all. He was also an original preacher and a gifted poet. Yet his vast learning never dimmed the flame of his evangelical zeal. On night he sat down and wrote these lines which apply to Pharaoh, to anyone who is hardening his heart against God and to all of us:

> There is a time, we know not when,
> A place we know not where,
> That marks the destiny of men
> To glory or despair.
>
> There is a line by us unseen,
> That crosses every path;
> The hidden boundary between
> God's patience and his wrath.
>
> Oh! where is that mysterious bourne
> By which our path is crossed;
> Beyond which, God himself hath sworn,
> That he who goes is lost.
>
> How far may we go on in sin?
> How long will God forbear?
> Where does hope end, and where begin
> The confines of despair?
>
> An answer from the skies is sent;
> "Ye that from God depart,
> While it is called to-day, repent,
> And harden not your heart!"

1. J. Addison Alexander, "The Hidden Line."

14

ONLY THIS ONCE—SAMSON

"And Samson called unto the Lord, and said, O Lord God, remember me, I pray thee, and strengthen me, I pray thee, only this once." (Judges 16:28)

The Philistines, the hereditary enemies of Israel and of God, were having a great celebration at Gaza, the capital of the kingdom. The celebration was in honor of their god Dagon. There were pantomimes, shows, and games, and the altars smoked with a thousand sacrifices. Their chief theme of rejoicing was that their god Dagon had delivered the mighty Samson, the Hebrew champion who had slain so many Philistines, into their hands. This, to them, was proof that Dagon was a mightier god than the God of Israel. When the people were well drunken, they began to shout and call for Samson to be brought forth and to exhibit his great strength. "Bring out Samson, the blind Hebrew giant! Hath not Dagon delivered him into our hands?" And here he comes! Poor, blind Samson, led by a little boy!

Like the births of John the Baptist and our Lord, the birth of Samson had been heralded by an angel. When he was born, they called him Samson—"Sunshine"—but now, alas, how dark was the night that had closed in on him. He had betrayed the secret of his great strength to the Philistines, who had bored out his eyes and harnessed him to the mill at Gaza. In Samson Agonistes, John Milton in one perfect line described the plight of Samson: "Eyeless in Gaza, at the mill with slaves."

Now here comes Samson, led by the lad! The spectators, crowding the roof garden of the temple and palace, commented with amazement upon the magnificent proportions of the blind giant. "Look at those legs like bronze pillars! And those shoulders like two hills! And that neck like a bull of Bashan! That back! Those great arms and hands! But now with his eyes out he is helpless!" Then they began to jeer, and taunt, and mock Samson: "Where is your Jehovah? Our Dagon is mightier than your God and has delivered you into our hands. Now you will slay no more of us with the jawbone of an ass! Today you will be our sport!" But beware, Philistines! Look at Samson's head! His hair has grown long again. Philistines, beware!

In the open court in front of the temple and palace, in full view of the three thousand people on the roof and the other thousands massed around the courtyard, Samson gave an exhibition of his strength, throwing great rocks over the buildings as if they were pebbles, snapping huge logs across his knees as if they were sticks, lifting enormous weights as if they were feathers. After a time he said to the lad who attended him, "I would like to rest for a little. Lead me over where there is some shade, perhaps at the entrance to the temple." Taking him by the hand, the lad led him to the arched entrance to the temple. There Samson stretched out his right hand until it encircled one of the pillars, and then his left hand till it embraced the pillar on the other side. There he stood reclining, with his head bowed down.

"Look at the giant," they called from the balconies. "Samson is tired. He has to rest for a little." But Samson was not resting. Samson was praying.

Suddenly he raised up his head and, turning his sightless balls heavenward, lifted up his voice in prayer: "O Lord God, remember me, I pray thee, and strengthen me, I pray thee, only this once."

One of the half-drunken Philistine women on the roof garden, feeling a slight tremor in the building, said to her companion, "What is happening? Is that an earthquake shock?" What was happening she never learned.

Suddenly, lifted out of their sockets by the mighty arms and shoulders and back of Samson, his muscles standing out like cables, the two pillars upon which he was leaning and which upheld the roof gave way, and down in one roar of ruin crashed the building, burying the multitude in its debris. When the yellow dust had settled, three thousand of the Philistines lay dead amid the ruins. And there among them lay Samson. God had heard his prayer.

"Only this once!" That was the remarkable thing in that final prayer of Samson, "O Lord, remember me and strengthen me, only this once." That phrase in Samson's prayer suggests the power of one sincere prayer, of one right decision, of one quick obedience to the Spirit of God, of one turning to God, one act of repentance. But it also suggests, on the other side, the power of one yielding to temptation, of one deception, of one evil deed, or false word, or wrong decision, one disobedience to the Holy Spirit.

THE "ONLY THIS ONCE" OF EVIL

The soul is the great thing in man. Great is the capacity of the soul for happiness, and great its capacity for suffering and for anguish: Samson himself is a striking example of the power of "only this once" for evil. Samson strangled a lion with his mighty hands, but he was not able to strangle his own physical nature. There is nothing new under the sun. In World War I and World War II the secret service on both sides made use of beautiful women to wrest military secrets from their enemies. Some times the Germans would employ such a woman, sometimes the French. Sometimes a woman of their nationality, sometimes of the enemy's nationality. Here we have the same thing. The Philistines knew that they were helpless in the presence of Samson until they had learned the secret of his great strength. In order to get that secret from him they employed this beautiful woman, Delilah, to get into the close friendship of Samson and thus learn from him the secret of his strength. Eleven hundred talents of silver were to be her reward.

It looked at first as if she would fail. But she was a persistent woman and, although a bad woman, a good Philistine patriot. At first Samson told her that if he was bound with seven green withes that had never been dried, he would be weak just like any other man. The seven green withes were procured; and while Samson slept on her lap, she wound them about his arms and his legs. Then she cried out, "The Philistines be upon thee, Samson!" When he heard that, Samson arose and broke the green withes as if they were threads of tow touched with fire, and then smote the Philistines.

The next time he came to visit her, Delilah reproached Samson for mocking her and again teased him to tell her the secret of his strength. This time Samson told her that if he was bound with new ropes that had never been used, he would be weak just like any other man. When she had bound him with the new ropes, Delilah called out to him, "The Philistines be upon thee!" At that Samson sprang up and broke the ropes as if they had been mere threads.

For the third time Delilah came back at him and asked him to tell her wherein his strength lay. This time Samson almost, but not quite, told that secret, for he told her that if the seven locks of his head were woven with the web, and fastened with the pin, he would be weak as any other man. But when Delilah had done this, and had driven the peg into the wall, and had shouted, "The Philistines be upon thee!" Samson awoke out of his sleep and, rushing upon the Philistines, carried dangling behind him beam and pin and web, and smote his enemies.

For the fourth time Delilah besought him to tell her the secret. She said to him, "How canst thou say, I love thee, when thine heart is not with me? thou hast mocked me these three times, and hast not told me wherein thy great strength lieth." Samson would not tell her at first. But when day after day she pressed him and urged him, and his soul was vexed and impatient, then he surrendered. Samson was a Nazarite from his mother's womb; that is, no razor or shears had ever come upon his head. He told Delilah that if his locks were cut and his head shaved, his strength would go from him. While he slept on her knees, a Philistine barber came and clipped off the seven golden locks. This time when she cried out, "The Philistines be upon thee, Samson!" Samson awoke and said to himself, "The Philistines! That's what I like to hear! I will go out as at other times and shake myself, and then shake them!" But, alas, Samson, this time you will not conquer. "And he wist not that the Lord was departed from him." The Philistines swarmed over him and quickly subdued him. They took him down to Gaza, to the prison house, where they bored out his eyes and bound his mighty arms and legs with fetters of brass; then they put a collar and hames on him, and hitched him like a beast to the pole of the mill. And there poor Samson went on his monotonous round, "Eyeless in Gaza, at the mill with slaves."

Three times Samson resisted the temptress, and it, looked as if he would be victorious over her. But the fourth time he surrendered and betrayed the secret of his strength. "Only this once," and Samson was done for.

For forty years, with magnificent courage and faith, Moses led the people through the wilderness on their journey out of Egypt to the Land of the Promise. But once, and only once, during that period Moses lost control of himself. When the people murmured and cried for water at Meribah, and God commanded Moses to smite the rock with his rod, Moses seized the rod and, crying out in anger, "Hear now, ye rebels; must we fetch you water out of this rock?" smote the rock, not once but twice. Now the long journey was over. There across the Jordan was the Promised Land, but all that Moses could do was to view it. He was not permitted to cross over because at Meribah, and only that once, he had failed to sanctify the Lord God before the people. By one act and one word of anger and passion many a soul has been kept out of the promised land of happiness and peace.

Esau was tired and hot and hungry as he came in from the hills and the fields that day, with the spoils of the chase hanging over his shoulders. As he drew near to the encampment, he smelled the savory stew that Jacob was preparing at the camp fire. He called on his brother to give him to eat of that stew. But the crafty Jacob said he would not give him to eat of the stew unless Esau, the older brother, would give him the birthright and the blessing that went with it. "What is my birthright to me?" said Esau. "Here I am, ready to perish with hunger. I can't eat my birthright. You take my birthright, and give me the stew." And the bargain was struck. Thus Esau despised his birthright. But later on when he found that Jacob had got not only the birthright but the blessing that went with it, then Esau in great distress and remorse went to Isaac and besought him to give him a blessing also. "Bless me, even me, also, O my father! Hast not thou one blessing reserved for me?" Too late, Esau! "Only this once," and you gave away the birthright and lost the blessing. Now you cannot have it back. "He found no place of repentance, though he sought it carefully with tears." How many descendants Esau has! "Only this once" to satisfy the appetite of a moment, and men have suffered a long remorse.

One evening as he walked on his roof garden, with the south wind beginning to blow softly, perhaps ready to indite a song and to set it to music with his lyre, David saw on another roof top a beautiful woman washing herself. In spite of the fact that she was another man's wife he took her into his palace for his own wife and cruelly and treacherously murdered her husband. David at length repented of his sin, when the man of God came to him and told him about that ewe lamb of the poor man which the rich man had seized and slaughtered to serve to his guests, and said, "Thou art the man!" David repented and was forgiven. But the prophet told him because his sin would make all the enemies of God to rejoice, the sword would never depart from his house. It never did. The sword flashed for the first time, and the little child for whose life David was pleading as he lay upon the ground was dead. The sword flashed again, and David's son, filthy Amnon, deflowered his sister Tamar. It flashed once again, and Absalom buried his dagger in the breast of Amnon. It flashed again, and Absalom rebelled against David and drove him from his throne. It flashed once again, and David, when he got the word from the Cushite runner that Absalom had fallen in the wood of Ephraim, wrapped his mantle about him and went up the winding stone stairs to the chamber over the gate and as he went thus he wept and lamented: "O my son Absalom, my son, my son Absalom! would God I had died for thee, O Absalom, my son, my son!" Only one look, David, that night on the roof garden, and ever since the sword of retribution has been flashing before your eyes and piercing into your heart.

In his *Confessions*, Augustine speaks of a young aristocrat who came from the same town in Africa. This young man, Alypius, had a boiling passion for the degrading scenes of the circus and coliseum. Through the influence of Augustine he gave up attendance upon the games and began to study truth with Augustine. But in Rome, where he had gone to study law, he was persuaded one day by some of his fellow students to go to the amphitheater. He told them that he would go with them, but that they could not force him to give either his mind or his eyes to such a spectacle. When the cruel battles between the gladiators were being fought, and the whole amphitheater was raging with excitement, Alypius kept his mind remote and his eyes closed; but at one loud roar of the blood-intoxicated mob, overcome by curiosity, but confident that he could resist now, even if he looked, he opened his eyes, and immediately was struck, as Augustine says, "with a deeper wound in his soul" than the gladiator had received in his flesh. He gazed, he shouted, he raved. He carried home with him a frenzy which goaded him to return, not only with those who had first dragged him thither, but before them in dragging over others in his turn. Only one look, and the young man was lost. If it is true, as the old hymn puts it, that "there is light for a look at the Crucified One," so also is there death for a look at evil and the evil one. "Turn away mine eyes from beholding vanity; and quicken thou me in thy way."

In the day of judgment when eternal destiny is allotted to the souls of men there will be many a one who will look back to an "only this once" one temptation consented to, one sinful decision, one evil deed, as the sin that ruined and condemned the soul.

THE "ONLY THIS ONCE" OF GOOD

We turn now to the brighter side as illustrated here by Samson at the very end of his life. It is the power for good of one decision, of one word, one prayer, one sincere repentance, and how it can cancel the sins of the past.

At first thought the life of Samson impresses one as a wasted life. But Samson never fell altogether away from God. He knew where the secret of his great strength lay. We take this final prayer of Samson as a token of his genuine repentance. In his life and in his death he rendered great service to the people of God. The writer of the epistle to the Hebrews puts Samson among the heroes of the faith :

> And what shall I say more? For the time would fail me to tell of Gideon and of Barak, and of Samson, and of Jephthah, of David also, and Samuel, and of the prophets: who through faith subdued kingdoms, wrought righteousness, obtained promises, stopped the mouths of lions.

The repentance of Peter shows us the power of only once turning to God. Only one denial of his Master led to three denials before the cock crew. But Peter received one look from Jesus. When Jesus, coming out of the judgment chamber, mocked and scourged, heard Peter's loud oaths of denial, he turned and "looked upon Peter." Immediately Peter went out and wept bitterly. That one act of sorrow and repentance restored him to his apostleship and made him forever and ever a power for good in the kingdom of God.

Paul had heaped persecution upon persecution and resistance upon resistance to the Holy Spirit. But on the road to Damascus he met Jesus and asked just one question, "Lord, what wilt thou have me to do?" Just one question of humility and faith out of the mouth of that cruel denier and persecutor of Jesus, and upon that question was built one of the grandest lives that the world has ever seen.

One act of anger and ingratitude separated the lost son of our Lord's great parable from his father's house. "Give me the portion of goods that falleth unto me," he said in anger one day to his father, "and let me depart from this place. I never want to see it again." That was the start. Just that once. But he added transgression to transgression, iniquity to iniquity, day after day, mile after mile, to the distance from his father's house. Until one day far down in a far country when he would fain have filled his belly with the husks that the swine did eat that lost son came to himself and said, "I will arise and go unto my father's house. . . . And he arose." Only that once of repentance, of prayer and action, and that carried him clear home, carried him clear through those towns through which he had passed on his way down, and where he had wasted his substance in riotous living. The women and evil men with whom he had consorted in those towns tried in vain to persuade him to stay with them. There were days, too, when he was as hungry as he had been when he envied the hogs their dinner. Yet he would not turn back, but went ever onward. There were days, too, when he must have said to himself, "My father may be dead, and that stern, hard elder brother of mine will be in control of the farm. He may turn the dogs on me and send me off." But in spite of all these difficulties and enticements and dangers he traveled ever onward, ever homeward, ever Godward, carried by the divine impulse of that "only this once" of his repentance.

The thief on the cross commenced a life of crime with one lawless and wicked act, and to it he added crime after crime and sin after sin until at length he hung on the cross, receiving the due reward of his misdeeds. There he hung, face black with the agony of approaching death, his body streaming with blood, his tongue cursing the King who hung next to him. But that was not the end of his history. He first rebuked the other thief, and then "only this once" turned his gaze toward the thorn-crowned Saviour and said, "Lord, remember me when thou comest into thy kingdom." "Only this once," and the angels of heaven rejoiced over him as Jesus brought him back into paradise with him, the first fruit of his Cross.

We should remember the dreadful power of an "only this once," of only one yielding, when we are confronted by temptation. The angels are watching over us to see what we will do and which way we will turn, whether they must weep over our wrong decision, or rejoice over our salvation.

There may be those who have yielded to some temptation and have slipped away from God. If so, hear the music of this great text, "Only this once." We are assured of the saving and restoring power of only one sincere prayer to God, "Hear me, I pray thee, and strengthen me only this once!" We are assured of the power of only one act of repentance, of only one look toward the crucified one. That prayer, that look, that cry, that repentance—and lo, the past is canceled. The stain of sin is washed out. The world's thought is summed up in the old proverb about the three things that never return—the shot arrow, the spoken word, and opportunity that has passed. All that the world knows is, "Whatsoever a man soweth, that shall he also reap." All that the world knows is, "What I have written I have written." But, thank God, that is not the gospel. The gospel proclaims the power of repentance, that God is gracious, that he will never turn away from those who turn to him, that he is able to save even unto the uttermost.

There is one more echo in that final prayer of Samson, "only this once," which I would like to awaken. We have seen the power of an "only this once" to undo the past and to bring a soul into the kingdom of God. But who knows how long one will have an opportunity to do that act, to make that repentance, to call upon God? Today may be an "only this once" of opportunity. When Jesus passed through Jericho, they all tried to silence poor blind Bartimaeus when he began to cry to Jesus to heal him. They all tried to keep him from coming to Jesus. He might have yielded to their threats and kept silent. He might have said, "I'll wait for some other day when there are not so many people around. I'll wait until the next time Jesus comes to Jericho." But there was no "next time." That was the last time Jesus passed through Jericho. It was the first chance and the last chance for Bartimaeus, and he made use of it. He called out, "Jesus, thou son of David, have mercy on me." And Jesus stood still. "Only this once," a cry like that, and the King of heaven stood still to listen! Jesus stood still, and the eyes of Bartimaeus were opened. "Only this once!" Jesus is passing again this way. Who will cry to him? Who will act in this day of grace and opportunity?

Years ago the "Stephen Whitney," a ship that carried emigrants to America from Ireland, ran on the rocks on the southern coast of Ireland. Her bow was right up against the cliff, and for a few minutes she hung there. The officers of the ship called out to the crew and the passengers to take advantage of that moment while the ship's bow was resting there on the cliff and get safely to shore. Some acted at once and were saved. Others were afraid and waited. In a moment the ship slipped off the cliff, and the rest went down to death with her in the boiling sea. "Only this once!" How great is its power! An "only this once" of repentance and prayer and decision for Christ can be stretched into an enternity of salvation and happiness.

15

ETERNAL MOTHERHOOD— RIZPAH

"And Rizpah the daughter of Aiah took sackcloth, and spread it for her upon
the rock, from the beginning of harvest until water dropped upon them
out of heaven, and suffered neither the birds of the air to rest on them
by day, nor the beasts of the field by night." (2 Samuel 21:10)

W hat a strange page this is—a page torn from the annals of
the reign of David; a page blotted with what to us seems to
be superstition, cruelty, and revenge; yet a page illuminated and
beautiful with a moving story of a mother's love and devotion, one
of the greatest ever written.

By nature David was a generous and magnanimous man. When
he received the tidings of the death of Saul, instead of rejoicing he
poured out his soul in that noble ode in which he praised Saul for
the virtues he possessed, in spite of his faults, and lamented over
the beloved Jonathan. After Saul's death in battle with the Philistines on Mount Gilboa, the house of Saul waxed weaker and
weaker, while the house of David, crowned king at Hebron, waxed
stronger and stronger. Saul's able captain of the host, Abner, had
been treacherously slain by David's great captain, Joab, and Saul's
son, Ishbosheth, had been assassinated by two of his own followers.
At length there was none left to dispute David's right to the throne.

Secure on his throne, David, had he followed the oriental cus-
tom and the example of other kings, would have celebrated his

triumph by a wholesale proscription and massacre of the followers of Saul. But instead of that what did David do? He summoned his ministers and said to them, "Is there yet any that is left of the house of Saul, that I may shew him kindness for Jonathan's sake?" His royal heart was filled with gratitude to God for fulfilling the promise made to him by Samuel and lifting him from the sheepfold to the throne of Israel.

When David was informed that there was left of Saul's line a lame grandson, Mephibosheth, the son of Jonathan, he had him brought to the court, and said to him, "I will surely shew thee kindness for Jonathan thy father's sake, and will restore thee all the land of Saul thy father; and thou shalt eat bread at my table continually." With that beautiful act of memory and mercy David began his reign.

Nevertheless David was a man of his day and generation. He was indeed "a man after God's own heart" in that, even in the dark chapters of his life, he never forgot God, and when God rebuked him for his sins he repented and said, "Against thee, thee only, have I sinned." Yet David was not altogether set free from the customs of his day and age, as we shall see in the tragedy of Rizpah and her sons.

Toward the end of David's reign there was a drought of three years' duration, with great distress and suffering. David inquired of the Lord—perhaps through prayer and sacrifice, perhaps by the Urim and Thummim, the mystic stones which flashed and gleamed upon the breastplate of the high priest—to learn the cause of the affliction of the drought. The answer he received was, "It is for Saul, and for his bloody house, because he slew the Gibeonites."

This mention of the Gibeonites carries us back to Joshua and the conquest of the land of Canaan. When the strongholds of Canaan were falling before the army of Joshua, the inhabitants of Gibeon, fearing they would perish like the people of the other towns, sent an embassy to wait on Joshua. When they appeared in the camp of Israel, the sacks on their asses were old and covered with dust; their wine vessels were rent and patched; their garments were faded and soiled; their bread was dry and moldy; and their shoes were bound on their feet with rags and ropes. They had all the appearance of men who had traveled a long distance. When Joshua asked them who they were and whence they came, they replied that they came from a very far country; that their people had heard of the God of Israel and the victories which Israel had won over the tribes on the other side of the Jordan; and that they had sent them to make a treaty of peace and alliance. Nothing doubting, Joshua made a covenant of peace with them and assured them they would suffer no harm from his army. But at the end of three days it was discovered that they did not come from afar, but from cities close by, and were themselves Canaanites. Duped and beguiled by this clever strategem, Joshua commanded his army to spare their cities but ordered that they should be hewers of wood and drawers of water for the camp of Israel.

Such then were the Gibeonites. In his day Saul, in his war against the Amorites—to which people the Gibeonites belonged— disregarded the covenant made with them by Joshua and sacked some of their towns and slew some of their people. It might seem to us today that there were many acts in the reign of Saul more culpable than this attack on the Gibeonites. But in the sight of God, Saul's deed was a heinous transgression because it involved the breaking of a solemn covenant, although that covenant had been secured by craft and fraud.

When David learned that the drought was a judgment upon Israel because of Saul's offense against the Gibeonites, he summoned their leaders and asked them what satisfaction and atonement he could make them for Saul's transgression. For answer the Gibeonites said that they did not ask for silver or gold from Saul's house, neither did they ask that David should punish any persons in Israel without regard to their connection with Saul and his house. Instead of that they asked that seven of the sons of Saul be delivered over to them to be "hung up before the Lord."

To this request David gave his consent. He spared Mephibosheth, Saul's grandson, son of Jonathan, because of his tender love for Jonathan, but chose seven others. Among them were the two sons of Rizpah, one of Saul's wives. These seven were delivered over to the Gibeonites, who "hung them up before the Lord." That is, their act was not a cold-blooded killing but, to them and to David, who gave his consent, a religious act, an offering to the Lord, an act of atonement for Saul's sin against the people of Gibeon when he broke the covenant Joshua had made with them.

We can imagine the sorrow and consternation there was in Rizpah's home that day when the officers of the king seized her two sons and carried them off to be hanged at Gibeon. But no tears or appeals could stay the decree of the king or save her sons from death. But as soon as the seven sons of Saul had been put to death, Rizpah left her home and journeyed to the barren hillside near Gibeon where the bodies of her two sons were hanging, exposed to the weather and to the birds and the beasts. There, hard by the tree or gallows upon which the bodies were hanging, Rizpah spread sackcloth on a great rock for a tent: and took up her sad and lonely vigil, a vigil which lasted from the beginning of barley harvest until the first rain. came at the end of the summer. Day and night she took her stand to defend the bodies of her sons. By day her waving cudgel drove off the circling birds and vultures, and by night her waving torch drove off the prowling jackal and wolf.

The word of her singular devotion spread throughout the land, and even the Gibeonites, who had demanded this sacrifice, must have been touched by such a spectacle When David heard of it—and perhaps he was troubled by what he had consented the went in person to Gibeon, took down the bodies of Rizpah's two sons and the five others, and gave them decent and honorable sepulture in the tomb of Saul's father, Kish, in the land of Benjamin.

It is not strange that Rizpah's beautiful, touching, and heroic devotion to the bodies of her dead sons has ever arrested the attention and held the admiration of those who read of it in the Bible, as it did that of David of old. Painters have devoted their imagination and their brushes to describe that lonely vigil of Rizpah, driving off the birds by day and the beasts by night from the suspended bodies of her sons; and poets have composed their songs to commemorate her devotion. Perhaps the most powerful poem that Tennyson ever wrote was his "Rizpah." It is the story of a poor English mother whose son had been hanged in chains for robbing the mails. When she went to see him before he was hanged, the keeper, in the midst of her interview, told her that the time was up and closed the door of the cell against her. As the door swung to, she heard her boy within cry, "O Mother!" Ever after the poor mother was hearing that last cry of her doomed boy, "O Mother!"

Wailing, wailing, wailing,
The wind over land and sea—
And Willy's voice in the wind,
"O mother, come out to me!"

When the mother was released from the madhouse where she had been confined because she was ever telling people that she was hearing her dead son call, "O Mother," she stole out by night and dug up one by one the bones of her son where they were buried beneath the gallows where he had been hanged in chains. Night after night, and one by one, she carried the bones to the churchyard, where she buried them in holy ground, close against the churchyard wall.

It is probable, too, that it was from this story of Rizpah that Kipling got his inspiration for his well-known lines,

If I were hanged on the highest hill,
Mother o' mine, O Mother o' mine'
I know whose love would follow me still,
Mother o' mine, O Mother o' mine.[1]

In the long annals of sacrificial motherhood we know of nothing more moving or more beautiful than Rispah's devotion. Only a mother would have done it. Her noble act is a picture, or symbol, of a mother's care for the bodies of her children, and still more for their souls. Not all mothers are strong, courageous, tender, and faithful like Rizpah; and not all mothers today are Christian mothers. Yet if all of us, once children, once sons and daughters, were only to a partial degree what our mothers trained us to be, what they hoped and prayed we might be, how much stronger and purer the homes of the land would be, how much stronger our churches, and how much better the world would be.

The appeal of this story is the appeal of tender memory of our own mothers; it is the appeal of gratitude and respect and affection. But it is more than that. It is an appeal to our souls. It is an appeal to our better selves. It is an invitation to godliness and worthy, unselfish living. It is an invitation to live for life hereafter

---

1. From Fudyard Kipling, "Mother o' Mine," *The Light That Failed.* Used by permission of Doubleday & Co. and Mrs. George Bambridge.

and everlasting, for the life to come is always reasonable, desirable, and necessary when one thinks of a godly mother.

Other memories perchance might fade and perish, but not the memory of mother. How many memories come back to us of a mother's patient toil and care, then taken as a matter of course; a mother's wise instruction, a mother's prayers, and, alas, a mother's grief and tears. Oh, how some whose mothers are no longer with them in this world would like to have them back, if only for a day or an hour, that they might atone to them for some hurt or sorrow or disappointment or neglect which a moment's thoughtlessness or carelessness or impatience gave to them!

Thaddeus Stevens was a Vermont boy who went down, to Pennsylvania and rose to high eminence in that state and in the nation; indeed, such an eminence that not a few have held that he was the strongest force in the government both during and just after the Civil War. The dust of Thaddeus Stevens, the great friend of the Negro, sleeps in a shabby neglected cemetery in the heart of the town of Lancaster, Pennsylvania. The epitaph on the grave, written by Stevens himself, tells why he is buried there, for it says that, finding that other cemeteries were restricted by charter rights and forbade the burial of Negroes in them, he had chosen to lie there where Negroes could be buried, so that even in death he might bear witness to those principles of equality and brotherhood which he had advocated through a long life.

Near Lancaster, too, is the grave of Thaddeus Stevens' mother, who did so much for her lame boy with his club foot when he was a child in Vermont. She resolved that in spite of his lameness he should not be handicapped in the race of life, and with great trial and sacrifice provided for him the means of an education. Recalling what his mother had done for him, Stevens wrote:

> I really think the greatest pleasure of my life resulted from my ability to give my mother a farm of two hundred and fifty acres, and an occasional gold piece, which she loved to deposit in the contributors' box of the Baptist church which she always attended.

Today there are roses blooming on her grave, for in his last will and testament Thaddeus Stevens, his mind going tenderly back to his mother's love and care, left a sum of money the income from which was forever to be used to plant each springtime "roses and other cheerful flowers" upon her grave.

Ah, yes! Those godly, all-loving, all-forgiving, all enduring, all-faithful mothers of ours! Both the living and those who died and, behold, are alive forevermore!

How like Rizpah of old on that barren rock near Gibeon where her sons were hanging, with staff and torch driving off the birds by day and the beasts by night, those mothers stood, and still stand, guard over not only our bodies, but our immortal souls—with the staff of their care and prayers, and the quenchless torch of their love, driving away by day the birds of doubt and unbelief, and by night the beasts of evil passions and thoughts which war against our souls!

Today many a son and many a daughter will lay "roses and other cheerful flowers" upon a mother's grave. I stood recently by a hilltop grave. On the hillside the dogwood was blooming as white and fair as of old. The spring flowers were appearing in the earth, and sweet melodious voices proclaimed that the time for the singing of birds had come once more. In the distance, between the hills, the river described its graceful winding as it flowed silently away, like the river of man's life.

Was it only a phantom of sanctifying memory or imagination? Or was it a reality, more real by far than other things in life? For as I stood there in meditation, and in memory's contemplation, I was conscious of the presence of another. Turning, I saw a stranger standing near. As he seemed to be waiting for me to speak, I said to him, "Friend, who art thou? And why dost thou intrude upon my sacred memories and reflections?"

At that, and with a slight accent of impatience and surprise in his voice, the stranger answered, "Dost thou not know me? I am the King of Terrors!" "The King of Terrors?" I replied; "I see nothing terrible about thee." Whereupon Death answered: "No; you see nothing terrible about me. In that thou speakest truly; for where mortals live and die as the one whose body in this grave lived and died, there I have no terrors at my command. It is only by the grave of those who have lived for this present world that I can rear my dread throne and dress it with such terrors as are at my command. But here, by the grave of such a mother as you recall this day, there is no sting which I can inflict and no victory which I can win. Farewell! I leave thee with thy memories of the sainted dead."

16

WHO SHALL COMMAND THE BATTLE?—AHAB

"Who shall order the battle? And he answered, Thou." (1 Kings 20:14)
"I have fought a good fight." (2 Timothy 4:7)

From an ancient battlefield outside the walls of Samaria where the Syrians fought against the army of Israel—a battlefield strewn with fallen pavilions, wrecked chariots, unlifted lances, shields which had been cast away, and, alas, strewn also with the dead—we can gather this timeless message: "Who shall order the battle? And he answered, Thou !"

With thirty-two tributary kings Ben-hadad, the king of Syria, inveterate foe of Israel, had invaded the land with a great army and was encamped before the walls of Samaria. He had come in such overwhelming force that Ahab, king of Israel, had no thought of resistance. To the Syrian's insolent demand for Ahab's treasure, his wives, and his children, Ahab answered, "O King, I am thine, and all that I have!" Not satisfied with thus humiliating Israel, Ben-hadad overreached himself and sent a second message, demanding that at a fixed hour Samaria be given over to pillage by the Syrian army. This was too much, even for Ahab. He called a council of the elders of Israel, to see

This sermon, entitled, "Life Is Your Battle," appeared in the *Pulpit Digest*, Dec., 1950. © 1950 by The Pulpit Digest Publishing Company.

What reinforcement he might gain from hope,
If not, what resolution from despair.[1]

With one voice the elders of Israel urged Ahab not to yield to the demand of Ben-hadad. "Hearken not unto him, nor consent." Ahab was a weak and wicked king, yet he had left a degree of respect for himself and his people. He told Ben-hadad that although he had consented to the first demand, this second demand he would not grant. "This thing I may not do!" Every man ought to have a "thus far and no further" in his character, a "this thing I may not do" to hurl at the tempter.

When Ahab's refusal was brought to him, Ben-hadad was beside himself with rage, and sent back to Ahab this threat: "The gods do so unto me and more also, if the dust of Samaria shall suffice for handfuls for all the people that follow me!" To this wicked threat Ahab made a wise answer, as far as we can tell, the only wise thing that Ahab ever uttered, but this time a proverb which has survived the vicissitudes of time and is just as powerful and pointed today as when it first fell from his resolute lips: "Let not him that girdeth on his harness boast himself as he that putteth it off." In other words, he said to Ben-hadad, "Before you hand out the dust of Samaria to your soldiers, first come and batter down her walls."

"And, behold, there came a prophet unto Ahab king of Israel." Ahab had been accustomed to the visits of the prophets of God. Hitherto they had come to warn him and denounce him for his sins. But now the prophet came to encourage him and strengthen him in the stand he had taken. Ahab had a bad record, and his wife, Jezebel, still worse. Together they had almost exterminated the prophets of Jehovah and the worship of God in Israel. But God has no grudges. When even the worst of men takes a stand for the truth, God gives him help. When a man stands on the side of the angels, the angels stand on his side.

The prophet and Ahab were standing together on the wall of beleaguered Samaria. The prophet said to Ahab: "Thus saith the Lord, Hast thou seen all this great multitude? behold, I will deliver it into thine hand this day; and thou shalt know that I am the Lord."

---

1. Milton, *Paradise Lost.*

But as the king stood on the battlements of the city and surveyed the great army of Ben-hadad, he felt a certain misgiving. There at the foot of the mountain, all around the walls of the city, lay the encircling host. Ahab saw their standards waving in the morning breeze. He could hear the neighing of the war horses, the rumbling of the chariots as they wheeled into position, and all the hum and murmur of the great host. He could see the flashing of the sun reflected on the helmets and shields and lances of Ben-hadad's army. No wonder that when the prophet said to him, "Hast thou seen all this great multitude? Behold, I will deliver it into thine hand this day," Ahab asked, "By whom?" The prophet answered that the victory would be won by the soldiers of the princes of the provinces; all told, seven thousand men. In astonishment Ahab said, "Who shall command the battle?"

And he answered, "Thou!"

Thus assured, Ahab mustered his little army of seven thousand, fell upon the Syrians at high noon when their captains were drinking themselves drunk in their pavilions, and smote them with a great slaughter.

There are three truths, all closely related, which are suggested by this battle outside the walls of Samaria: first, that life is a battle; second, that life is your battle; and third, that the battle is the Lord's.

LIFE IS A BATTLE

Some of the great masters of imagination, like Edmund Spenser or John Bunyan, have generally thought of life under two metaphors, a pilgrimage or a battle. This is true also of the Bible. Sometimes it speaks of life as a journey, a pilgrimage. But more often, perhaps, it speaks of life as a battle, a warfare, which is not accomplished until life is over. In this warfare some are only recent recruits. All they know about the battle is the music of the bands, the cheering of the people, the waving of the banners in the sunlight. Others are in the midst of the warfare, standing in the very forefront of the hottest battle, their uniforms stained and torn, caked with mud and blood, their faces blackened with powder. Others, again, are nearing the end of the battle, their armor well hacked and dented with the blows of the foe. Soon for them will sound the trumpet of recall. But for one and all life is a battle. Is there not a warfare appointed unto the sons of men?

When a royal infant is born, his name is at once inscribed on the roll of one of the regiments of the army. So every man is born, as it were, on a battlefield. When you look upon the face of a newborn babe, with so much love and care and hope hovering about him, sometimes you will remember that this child has entered the lists in the battle of life. For him there can be no exemption. In this warfare there is no discharge. The puzzle of life begins the moment we forget that life is a battle; not an end in itself, but a field of battle, a warfare where you are trained and tested for the life which is to come. In *Tom Brown's School Days* the author speaks of the influence of Thomas Arnold of Rugby over the boys at that school, and how he impressed on their minds the fact that they were entering life as a battlefield, that "it was no fool's or sluggard's paradise into which he had wandered by chance, but a battlefield ordained from of old, where there are no spectators, but where the youngest must take his side and the stakes are life and death."

LIFE IS YOUR BATTLE

That warfare cannot be undertaken for you by anyone else. In the American Civil War a drafted man could be released from service by paying the sum of three hundred dollars for a substitute; but in this battle of life all the gold of Ophir cannot purchase you a substitute. You are drafted at birth, and to the front you must go. No love, no sheltering, no intercessory prayer on the part of those interested in you, can deliver you from the battle. When the tidings came to David as he stood there waiting by the tower during the battle in the wood of Ephraim, that Absalom had fallen in battle, and the second runner had said to David, "The enemies of my lord the king, and all that rise against thee to do thee hurt, be as that young man is," David wrapped his mantle about him and went up the stone stairs to the chamber over the gate, and as he went thus he lamented, "O my son Absalom, my son, my son Absalom! would God I had died for thee! O Absalom, my son!"

David was wishing there for the impossible; that he might have taken Absalom's place in the midst of battle and had died in that tangled wood instead of his son. But that is always impossible. No father, no mother, no husband, no wife, no son, no daughter, no brother, no sister, no nearest friend, can fight another's battle. Even the Son of Man had to fight his battle alone. In his human nature he yearned for fellowship and companionship in that dread struggle, and asked the three disciples to watch with him. But even that was not granted him. He had to drink his cup and fight his battle alone. "I have trodden the winepress alone." It cannot be otherwise with us.

The fact that life is a battle and that every man must fight his own battle ought to teach us sympathy one for the other. If the veil which screens the innermost lives of those who make up a single congregation could be lifted, how many difficulties, battles, sieges, anxieties, trials, burdens, sorrows, temptations, disappointments, we could see!

In this battle every man is his own commander in chief. When Ahab asked, "Who shall order the battle?" the prophet answered, "Thou!" In this warfare of the soul, in this campaign of life, you are not a private soldier, an officer, or a noncommissioned officer, but the commander in chief. You alone can order the battle. In this struggle we engage with the powers of evil. As Paul put it, "We wrestle not against flesh and blood, but against principalities, against powers, against the rulers of the darkness of this world."

In this ancient battle between Samaria and Israel, the record is that the Israelites "slew every one his man." Each soldier picked out his adversary and fought against that one. This is what we ought to do in the battle of life. In this struggle we are to isolate our adversary and fight it out with him to the bitter end. So the apostle says to "lay aside every weight, and the sin which doth so easily beset us." All men have their weights in the race of life and their own besetting sin. With one, a bad temper. With another, a sharp or slanderous tongue. With another, diseased imagination. With another, pride or sloth, or avarice, or envy, or jealousy, or an evil appetite. These are the foes which we must cut out from the ranks of the enemy and with them do our battle.

Then there are enemies of another sort, a different kind of adversary altogether: sickness, a thorn in the flesh, a frustrated hope or ambition, domestic unhappiness, the burden of sorrow or loneliness. But no matter who the adversary or the invader may be, the battle is yours. "Who shall order the battle? Thou!" If you do not, no one else will do it for you.

The Battle Is the Lord's

Ahab was told that he must command in the battle, and yet was given the assurance that when he did so, the Lord would give him the victory.

When Jehoshaphat stood in battle against the hosts of Moab and Ammon, one of the Levites upon whom the Spirit of the Lord had come spoke to the king and the army, "Thus saith the Lord, Be not afraid nor dismayed by reason of this great multitude; for the battle is not yours, but God's."

When the famous Field Marshal Montgomery was asked as a young officer what he would do when confronted with a certain military situation, he answered, "I would first pray about it, and then I would fight." That is what we ought to do in the battle of life. We should seek God's guidance and help, but at the same time do our own part and fight the battle which is appointed unto us.

In another war between these same ancient enemies, Israel and Syria, the prophet Elisha was once surrounded in Dothan by a great host of the enemy. When his servant went up on the wall early in the morning and heard the hum of this host and saw their infantry and chariots drawn up in battle array, he cried out, "Alas, my master! how shall we do?"

But Elisha prayed for the young man, "Lord, open his eyes, that he may see." And when his eyes were opened, he saw the mountain round about him was full of chariots and horses of fire. Always about us in our battle for evil when we fight on the Lord's side is this mighty, if invisible, reinforcement, the heavenly host.

For all of us is this message, this ringing, soul-stirring message from the Bible, "Who shall order the battle? And he answered, Thou!" Thou! Thou with all thy sacredness. Thou with all thy capacity. Thou with all thy value to God. Thou with all thy influence upon thy fellow men. Thou with all the glory that is laid up for thee. Upon thy sword is inscribed the word, "Thou"; and upon the crown of life which is laid up for thee, and which God would place upon thy brow, on that is the word written, "Thou!" How splendid, then, is that final message of the great warrior and apostle of Christ, "I have fought a good fight. . . . Henceforth there is laid up for me a crown."

The Jews have a tradition that when Lucifer was cast out of heaven he was asked in hell what he missed most out of his former life. He replied, "I miss most the sound of the trumpet in the morning." Does anyone miss the note of the trumpet? Has the spirit been ebbing, and the high moral and courageous purpose been wavering? Then hear this trumpet note from the prophet of God, "Who shall order the battle? And he answered, Thou!"

In *Pilgrim's Progress* when Mr. Valiant-for-truth received his summons to go over the river, he said:

> "My sword I give to him that shall succeed me in my pilgrimage, and my courage and skill to him that can get it. My marks and scars I carry with me, to be a witness for me that I have fought His battles Who now will be my rewarder." As he stepped into the river, he said, "Death, where is thy sting?" and as he went down deeper, "Grave, where is thy victory?" So he passed over, and all the trumpets sounded for him on the other side!

17

THE REACTION OF
REVENGE—HAMAN

*"So they hanged Haman on the gallows that he had
prepared for Mordecai."* (Esther 7:10)

About two thousand years ago a man going early to work in a
vineyard in the suburbs of Shushan, the capital of Persia,
passed down one of the avenues and saw hanging from a gallows
near the royal palace a man's body. The body was swaying to and
fro with the morning wind, and vultures were beginning to circle
around it. As he stood looking at this body hanging from the
gallows, another workman came along, and he said to him, "Whose
body is that hanging from the gallows?"

The man answered, "That is the body of Haman."

"What!" exclaimed the other. "You don't mean Haman, the
king's viceroy and prime minister, who lived in yonder palace with
the carved lions at the gate?"

"Yes," said the other, "it is the body of Haman, the king's
minister. He built the gallows for the hanging of the Jew Mordecai,
the foster father of the queen. But the king yesterday commanded
that Haman himself be hanged on the gallows which he had built
for Mordecai."

"So they hanged Haman on the gallows that he had prepared for Mordecai." That was the reaction of Haman's plot
for revenge.

The book of Esther is one of the most striking, readable, and dramatic books in the Bible. With its gorgeous palaces and its royal banquets it seems like a page from The Arabian Nights. In Esther men rise and fall; the proud are brought low, and the humble are exalted. Princes and nobles drink and revel, while the common people are perplexed. Plots and conspiracies are hatched and frustrated. Love, hate, pride, fear, revenge, faith—all these passions and emotions, worthy and unworthy, which sweep with their winds the souls of men, appear here in unforgettable incarnation. This is one of the two books of the Bible in which the name of God does not appear. But although God's name is not here, his providence, his sovereignty, and his truth appear on every page.

Let us look for a moment at the background of this great story. Because she would not go into the banquet of Ahasuerus, the Xerxes who invaded Greece and was defeated at Salamis, and display her beauty to the king's drunken princes and nobles, Vashti the Queen was set aside; and the beautiful Jewess Esther, put forward by her cousin and foster father Mordecai, was elevated to the throne. About the same time Haman was promoted to the second place in the Persian empire. He undoubtedly won this post by his great ability as an administrator. Like so many other great national leaders, Haman did not belong to the nation which he ruled as viceroy of the king, for he was not a Persian but an Amalekite, a people hostile to the Jews and despised by them. Napoleon was not a Frenchman, but an Italian Corsican; Hitler was not a German, but an Austrian; Stalin is not a Russian, but a Georgian. So Haman, the second man of the Persian empire, was not a Persian but an Amalekite. He is one of the most sharply etched characters in the Bible and certainly one of the ugliest— monstrous in pride, hate, revenge, conspiracy, and appalling in his final fate and judgment. Yet there are things about Haman which we can all study with profit, as we see him hanging there in the morning light from that gallows which he had built for Mordecai, fifty cubits high.

When Haman was elevated to his lofty post, everyone did him reverence. When he came down the steps of the royal palace, or drove along the avenue in Shushan, all men bowed before him and did him honor. All but one; and that one was the Jew Mordecai, the queen's foster father. This one exception to the chorus of praise and reverence with which Haman everywhere was greeted filled him with mortification and rage. It cast a shadow over all his fame and splendor. It was the one fly in his ointment, which, as the wise man said, "causeth the whole ointment to stink." We are not told just why it was that Mordecai refused to bow to Haman. Perhaps they had had some personal difference. Perhaps because Haman was an Amalekite, and was hostile to the Jews. Perhaps he wore upon his garments or upon his uniform some image or symbol of idolatry, and for that reason, as a believing Jew, Mordecai refused to bow down. Whatever his reason, it was a conspicuous and splendid instance of independence and courage, for the general habit or tendency is to bow down to and honor those who are honored by others.

The Folly of Permitting One Thing to Ruin Happiness

The first important truth which is preached by that body dangling there from the gallows with the vultures wheeling round it, is the folly of permitting one thing to ruin happiness and poison the soul. That was the first great mistake that Haman made. It was the first link in the chain of ruin which he forged for himself. Here was a man who had great honor, fabulous wealth, and far-flung possessions. From India to the Aegean Sea there was a long line of bowing princes and satraps. There was only one exception, and that was this Jew Mordecai. Haman forgot the thousands of others and saw only the unbowing Mordecai. From the Black Sea and the Caspian Sea and the Caucasian Mountains on the north, clear down to Arabia and the Numidian deserts in Africa, there was not a palace, a garden, a grove, a slave, or a ship which Haman could not have had for the asking. Yet there he was, all distressed and cut to the heart because one comparatively obscure Jew would not bow down when he passed! All this, Haman said, referring to his riches and splendor and glory, "availeth me nothing, so long as I see Mordecai the Jew sitting at the king's gate."

Supreme folly! The one thing Haman could not have spoiled the pleasure and satisfaction of everything that he did have. It was by indulging in that same folly that the world went astray in the beginning. The man and the woman were placed in that beautiful garden which was well watered by the four branches of the river which flowed through it. There grew every tree that was pleasant to the sight and good for food. All these pleasures the man and the woman were permitted to enjoy. There was just one thing that was forbidden them, and that was to eat of the tree of the knowledge of good and evil. But the man and the woman passed by all the other trees, so good to look upon and so delightful for food, and gave their whole attention to the one tree that was forbidden them; and, under the seductive insinuations of the tempter and his false promises, ate of that tree and were driven out of the garden. How often that history has been repeated. The centering of thought and desire upon one thing not granted, one forbidden tree, has turned men and women out of the garden of peace and contentment. One thing unpossessed and impossible has spoiled great realities and great possibilities. One unbowed head hides a thousand friendly countenances. That happens sometimes in the social world. Hearts are filled with bitterness and unrest because, although a hundred doors are opened to them, one door has an unwelcome sign over it. It happens in the world of artists and singers. The one dissenting note of disparagement or criticism casts into discord the praise of others. It happens in the world of letters. One unkind or unfavorable review is a thorn in the spirit of an author, and he forgets the numerous friendly and favorable reviews. Cleopatra, the enchantress of the Nile, cast her spell over Mark Antony and over Julius Caesar; but when she was repulsed by the cold Octavius, afterward Caesar Augustus, she put the asp to her bosom. So it goes in life. Souls brood over one act of discourtesy and unkindness. They are angry and displeased because one apple of desire is beyond their reach.

The far wiser course is to rejoice in what you have and waste no tears of longing or regret or disappointment over what is forbidden. Take the positive in life, and forget the negative. Think upon those who love you, and forget those who do not. Shakespeare makes Hamlet say, "There is nothing either good or bad, but thinking makes it so." This is only a half truth because there are some things that are good and some things that are bad, no matter what you think about them. Yet it is true that things in themselves trivial and insignificant, dwelt upon and brooded over, at length assume colossal and terrible proportions which are altogether unreal.

THE FOLLY AND REACTION OF REVENGE

The second truth that is inscribed as on a placard on that body of Haman hanging on Mordecai's gallows is the folly and reaction of revenge. It was bad enough that Haman permitted the slight put upon him by Mordecai to shadow and dim all his possessions and destroy his peace of mind, but what followed was much worse. His wounded vanity and pride brought forth hate, and hate brought forth revenge, and attempted revenge brought forth degradation, ruin, and death. Haman planned to revenge himself on Mordecai, and what a revenge it was to be! He scorned to destroy Mordecai alone, but conceived and brought forth the worst and most dangerous plot against the people of Israel that the world has ever seen until the days of Hitler and the terrible concentration camps where the Jews perished by the hundreds of thousands. He planned to destroy Mordecai; but Mordecai was to perish in a massacre which would take the life of the whole Jewish people.

With this in mind Haman went to the king and, without giving the name of the people, said to him,

> There is a certain people scattered abroad and dispersed among the people in all the provinces of thy kingdom; and their laws are diverse from all people; neither keep they the king's laws: therefore it is not for the king's profit to suffer them. If it please the king, let it be written that they may be destroyed.

Xerxes, probably well saturated with drink, apparently did not take the trouble to inquire who these dangerous people were, but took the signet ring from his finger and gave it to Haman, telling him to get out his decree of destruction and extermination and sign and stamp it with the royal ring. This Haman did, and sent out the decree by fast posts into all parts of the vast empire of Persia, that on the thirteenth day of the twelfth month, Adar, all Jews—male and female, young and old, little children and women— were to be slain. Then Haman, well pleased with the easy assent he had won from the king to his ferocious plot and conspiracy, "sat down with the king to drink; but the city Shushan was perplexed."

Now enters the unnamed actor, the final disposer of all human events, that God whose name is not spoken or written in this book. Moved by the earnest appeal of Mordecai, who told her that she had come to the kingdom for such a time as this, that she might deliver her people from death, Esther, unbidden and unsummoned, went in to the presence of Ahasuerus to plead for her people. When she touched the top of the scepter which was in his hand, the king said to her, "What wilt thou, queen Esther? and what is thy request? It shall be given thee to the half of the kingdom." Esther did not then tell the king what her chief purpose and desire were, but merely requested that the king invite Haman to come that day to the banquet which she had prepared. Haman was highly elated that he was so honored by the queen. The only man in the empire, after the king himself, who was invited to the banquet! But as he went out from the banquet that evening, proud and happy, and with a glad heart, and was going down the palace steps, he saw something which cast a dark shadow over his joy and poisoned all his happiness. It was the Jew Mordecai, who did not rise to greet him and salute him when he passed.

When he got home to his own palace that evening, Haman told his friends and Zeresh his wife that he had gone to the queen's banquet; and that when he was leaving the royal palace Mordecai had refused to bow before him. "What," he said, "are all my children and riches and princes and slaves and all my honors, so long as I see Mordecai the Jew sitting at the king's gate?" Unfortunately for him Haman had a wife, Zeresh, who suggested to him the next step in his downfall and ruin. She was a wife like Jezebel, who, when Ahab came home to his palace unhappy and out of sorts because he could not persuade Naboth to sell him the vineyard which he coveted, told him to have Naboth arraigned on false charges and then stoned, so that he could take possession of his vineyard. She was like Macbeth's wife, who said to that hesitating soldier, "Infirm of purpose, lend me thy dagger!" So Zeresh spoke to her husband Haman. She said in effect, "Who are you, Haman? Are you not the viceroy of the king? Are you not the second man in the great empire of Persia? And yet you permit a little Jew to stand in your way and spoil your happiness! I will tell you what to do. Build a gallows fifty cubits high. Then speak to the king tomorrow and secure his permission to hang Mordecai on the gallows. Then tomorrow you can go in merrily with the king to the second banquet."

Haman said to his wife and friends, "That is the very thing! It shall be done!" Summoning his servants, he ordered them to secure carpenters and begin the erection that very night of the gallows fifty cubits high.

That night the sound of the hammers rang out on the royal avenue as Haman's carpenters built the gallows on which Mordecai was to be hanged. But now comes this sentence in this book without the name of God; this great sentence concerning God's providence: "On that night could not the king sleep." Had it been the night before, or the night after, that the king was afflicted with insomnia, all would have been different. Mordecai would have been hanged, and the Jews would have perished. But it was on that very night when the gallows was building that the king could not sleep. In his restlessness he called in his secretaries and bade them entertain him by reading from the chronicles of his reign. As one of them was reading from these chronicles, he came to a paragraph which related how two of the king's chamberlains had conspired to assassinate him, but that the plot was exposed by Mordecai, and thus the king's life was saved. As he listened to that, the king suddenly was all interest and attention. "Read that again!" he said. When he heard it the second time, he said, "Was anything ever done to honor that man for saving my life?"

The secretaries answered, "Nothing, your majesty."

The king's sleepless night had now worn to the morning, and the sun had risen over the river Ulai, the scented groves and garden, and the royal palaces of Shushan. A messenger came to the king to announce that Haman, who had come early to get the king's consent to the hanging of Mordecai, was in the outer court. When he heard that his prime minister was there, Ahasuerus said, "Let him come in." When he came in, the king said to Haman, "Haman, I learned last night that there is a man who once did me a great service. I would like to do something to recognize him and honor him. You are a man of fertile suggestions, Haman. What do you think should be done unto the man whom the king delighteth to honor?"

When Haman heard this, he thought in his heart, "The man whom the king delighteth to honor! And who can that be but

Haman? Whom would the king delight to honor more than my-self?" Then he answered the king and said, "I will tell you what to do, your Majesty, for the man whom you delight to honor. Bring forth the royal apparel, and also the royal crown. Let the man be clothed in the king's robes, and let the king's crown be set upon his head. Then have the king's charger brought out of the stable and saddled and bridled with the golden bit and the royal caparison be put on him. Then have the man whom you delight to honor mounted on the horse, and command one of the princes of the kingdom to take the horse by the bridle and lead him through the streets of the city, calling out as he goes, 'Thus shall it be done unto the man whom the king delighteth to honor.'"

The king looked at the cruel and crafty Haman for a moment and then said, "Haman, thou hast well spoken. Thou art the prince to lead the horse, and Mordecai is the man who will ride the horse."

When the parade was over and Haman returned, crestfallen, humiliated, and frightened, to his own palace, his wife and friends told him that his doom now was certain. When he went with heavy heart to the second banquet, it was only to hear the queen expose the plot against her people and point out "this wicked Haman" as the author of the plot. The outraged king at once gave command that Haman be put to death. As they were leading him out, one of the attendants turned and said to the king, "Your majesty, how shall we put Haman to death? Last night he built a gallows fifty cubits high for the hanging of Mordecai."

"Hang him thereon," said the king. And that was the end of Haman. That was how it was that the workman, going early to work in the vineyard in the suburbs of the city, saw a body hanging from the gallows, swaying slightly in the morning wind, with the vultures wheeling over it.

Such was the reaction of Haman's revenge. The slight that Mordecai had put upon him, passed over, ignored, would have permitted him to live and die in peace and honor. Wounded pride and vanity are always dangerous. They not only dim the light of the sun, but tempt to sin.

In 1800 the Democrats—or Republicans, as they were then known—put Jefferson and Burr at the head of their ticket. At that time electors voted only for president, and the second highest in the electoral college became vice-president. Jefferson and Burr each received seventy-three votes in the electoral college. This threw the election into the House of Representatives. On the thirty-sixth ballot, Jefferson was chosen president, and Burr became vice-president. One of the determining factors in the defeat of Burr was the influence of Alexander Hamilton with the Federalists, who held the balance of power in the House of Representatives. Hamilton wrote letters in which he said that Burr had "formed himself upon the model of Cataline." In a letter to Bayard of Delaware, Hamilton wrote, "I could scarcely name a discreet man of either party in our state who does not think Mr. Burr the most unfit man in the United States for the office of President."

Because of what Hamilton had said about him, and also because of what he said in the campaign for the governorship of New York in 1804, Burr determined to have his revenge and called Hamilton out. But that fatal shot on the "tragic shores of Weehawken" not only ended Hamilton's life, but ended the career, and also the happiness of Burr. Henceforth he was a fugitive and vagabond upon the face of the earth. Long afterward Burr confessed that it would have been wiser for him to have taken the sensible view that the world was big enough for both Aaron Burr and Alexander Hamilton.

"Behold, how great a matter a little fire kindleth." Malice blots out life's perspective. Woe to him who spreads his sails to that wind. Wise, therefore, was the injunction of the apostle, "Be ye angry, and sin not: let not the sun go down upon your wrath: neither give place to the devil." The man who harbors ill feeling against his fellow man, or who plans to get even or have revenge, is doing what Haman did, giving "place to the devil." Jesus taught us a far better way when he said, "Ye have heard that it hath been said, Thou shalt love thy neighbour, and hate thine enemy. But I say unto you, Love your enemies, bless them that curse you, do good to them that hate you, and pray for them which despitefully use you, and persecute you; that ye may be the children of your Father which is in heaven."

18

THE SOUL'S ADVOCATE—ABIGAIL

"Bound in the bundle of life." (1 Samuel 25:29)

Springtime in Palestine. "The winter is past, the rains are over and gone; the flowers appear on the earth; the time of the singing of birds is come, and the voice of the turtle is heard in the land." There was a softness in the air, the indefinable breath of nature's revirescence. The valleys and hills were green with the new grass. But here and there were patches of white in the midst of the green—not snow still lingering on the hillside, but flocks of sheep being led to the shearing ground. We shall visit this one flock of three thousand sheep. Not only sheep were gathered here, but goats and cattle and asses and camels. Multitudes of children, too, and the women with their picturesque headdresses of vivid blue, yellow, and red. The fires were burning where the oxen were spitted and roasted for the feast, for sheep shearing was a time of social joy and rejoicing, of eating and making merry, and of giving and receiving gifts—just like the old-time harvest homes and barn-raisings in America.

The sheep were first washed in the pool and then led up to the shearing platforms, where you could see the flash of the shearing knives and hear the bleating of the sheep. As one by one the sheep of this flock of three thousand were sheared and sent away, the heaps of white wool rose higher and higher. Seated under a pavilion was the lord and master of this domain. His name was Nabal, a degenerate descendant of the great family of Caleb, Joshua's heroic companion. Nabal was called a "great" man—not great, however, in personality and moral character, but merely great in the number of his flocks and herds. But his most valuable possession, although Nabal did not appreciate or realize it, was his beautiful and accomplished wife, Abigail. This beautiful woman was married to the hard-drinking churl and boor Nabal. This therefore was one of the first editions of *The Beauty and the Beast.*

As Nabal sat viewing with satisfaction the scene of the sheep shearing and watched the heaps of wool rise higher and higher, three young men approach his pavilion. Bronzed by wind and sun, and toughened by long marches, these three young men belonged to David's band of six hundred. At that time David was hiding in the forests around Carmel, where he had taken refuge from the insane and jealous fury of King Saul. Wherever his men went as they roamed over the hills near Carmel, they came upon the flocks of Nabal, which they never molested, but which they guarded from robbers and from wolves. They reported to David that Nabal was shearing his sheep; and since this was a time for good cheer and the giving and receiving of gifts, they asked permission to go to Nabal and ask for a present for David and his men. This was the errand that brought them to Nabal.

When Nabal heard their request he said, "David? Who is David?. . . I never heard of him! But I have heard of a band of robbers and runaway slaves who have been lurking in our mountains and robbing our people. Tell your David that I have better use to make of my bread and flesh and wine than to waste it on a gang of marauders."

David, we are told, was a man of "ruddy countenance." But when the three young men brought that churlish answer from Nabal, David's countenance was white—white with anger and rage. He gave a signal to his bugler to sound a blast on the trumpet. As soon as the trumpet sounded, his six hundred men, veterans of many a march and campaign, came pouring out of their dens and caves, down from the hillsides, and out of the woods and the thickets. Choosing four hundred of them and leaving two hundred to guard his camp, David commanded every man to gird on his sword and start the march towards Carmel and Nabal. As he marched along, David was saying to himself, and perhaps aloud, "Nabal doesn't know, does he, who David is? And never heard of the son of Jesse? Well, he'll know who he is before this time tomorrow. Nabal thinks we are a band of outlaws and robbers, does he? Well, then, we'll teach him what robbers and outlaws can do! God do so and more also to me, if, by the morning light, there remaineth of Nabal's household and tribe a single man alive!" So the march of revenge commenced, every man's sword clanking in its scabbard. March! March! March! Clank! Clank! Clank!

Meanwhile servants had told Abigail of the insult which Nabal had hurled at David. Ere long some of the shepherds of the hills came in with the tidings that David and four hundred of his men were marching on Carmel. Abigail knew what that meant. She might have said to herself, "Nabal has made his bed; let him lie in it. David will give him what he deserves. And when that happens, I shall be free of a cruel, wicked, boorish husband." But instead of that, Abigail acted quickly to do what she could to save Nabal from destruction, and all the innocent people who would have perished with him.

The asses were laden with loaves of bread, dressed sheep, parched corn, cakes of figs, clusters of raisins, and bottles of wine. With these presents for David and his men Abigail set off in the direction from which she knew David would be coming. All through the night the two processions were marching. In the morning just as the sun was gilding the slopes of Carmel "at the covert of the hill," a little valley between two peaks, the two processions met— the procession of vengeance and blood, and the procession of reconciliation and mercy. As Abigail dismounted from her beast and knelt before the uncrowned king of Israel, David and his four hundred men came to a halt.

If a list were made of the ten most eloquent speeches of the Bible, at the top of the list perhaps would be Paul's beautiful farewell address to the elders of the church of Ephesus at Miletus. High also would rank Judah's moving appeal to Joseph in Egypt, pleading with him not to retain Benjamin as a hostage: "It shall come to pass, when he seeth that the lad is not with us, that he will die; and thy servants shall bring down the gray hairs of thy servant our father with sorrow to the grave." Near the top, too, of this list of the ten greatest speeches would stand this address which the lovely Abigail made to David. She began by taking the blame for Nabal's insult upon herself. "Upon me, my lord, upon me let this iniquity be." If she had been there, she said, it would have been otherwise. Another kind of answer would have been rendered, and a present would have been given. Then she told David that he ought not to pay attention to Nabal's insult. "He is a son of Belial. Nabal is his name [which means fool] and folly is with him. He is not worthy of your anger or vengeance."

Then Abigail struck the note of God's great purpose in David's life. God had appointed David to rule over Israel. His was to be a "sure house," and the Lord would fight his battles for him. Then she struck the great note of God's providence. What God had promised he would fulfill. The enemies of David would be slung out as if from "the middle of a sling," but the soul of David should be "bound in the bundle of life with the Lord thy God."

Because this was so, Abigail appealed to David not to do what he was on the way to do; not to stain his life with bloodshed and slaughter. And then, exercising a woman's prerogative, and assuming that David had already yielded to her entreaty, she said to him, "This shall be no grief unto thee, nor offense of heart unto my lord, either that thou hast shed blood causeless, or that my lord hath avenged himself."

It was no wonder that David yielded to this beautiful plea on the lips of a beautiful woman. With all his faults, which were many, David was always a man who was ready to give heed to the Higher Voice when it spoke to him, whether to warn him from contemplated sin or rebuke him for sins he had already committed. "When thou saidst, Seek ye my face; my heart said unto thee, Thy face, Lord, will I seek." There was David at his best! When Abigail had finished her plea, David said to her: "Blessed be the Lord God of Israel, which sent thee this day to meet me; And blessed be thy advice, and blessed be thou, which hast kept me this day from coming to shed blood, and from avenging myself with mine own hand. For in very deed, as the Lord God of Israel liveth, which hath kept me back from hurting thee, except thou hadst hasted and come to meet me, surely there had not been left unto Nabal by the morning light a single man."

When Abigail returned home she said nothing to Nabal of what had transpired, for he was dead drunk. But the next morning when the wine was gone out of him, she told him what had happened. And then, either because of rage at Abigail and the

giving of gifts to David and his men or for fear, when he realized
the doom he had narrowly escaped, Nabal suffered a stroke and
died. "His heart died within him, and he became as a stone." All of
which tells us that vengeance belongs to God. He knows how to
deal with evildoers. It was better that Nabal should have been
judged by God than by David. Perhaps David remembered this
incident when he wrote his wise sentence in the Psalms, "Fret not
thyself because of evil-doers."

In Abigail's wonderful speech there is one phrase which stands
out as a jewel of surpassing beauty, "Bound in the bundle of life."
This is a metaphor belonging to the days when men carried their
most valued treasures, not in a trunk or a suitcase, but wrapped
up—bound up in the center of a bundle. This is a phrase that
sounds sweetly across the years for me, for often did I hear it on
the lips of my father at the family altar as he prayed for his children that they might be "bound in the bundle of life," not only for
this life, but for the life to come, with the Lord their God. This
phrase tells us that God's providence binds us about and protects
us.

GOD'S PROVIDENCE IN OUR LIFE

The truth which Abigail so eloquently expressed to David when
she pleaded with him to hold back his hand from blood because
he was "bound in the bundle of life" she had already applied to her
own life. It was a hard, sad lot for a gifted and beautiful woman
like Abigail to have for a husband a cruel, churlish sot like Nabal.
It would be difficult to imagine a more painful lot. But Abigail did
not permit this misfortune to embitter her, sour her spirit, or turn
her away from God. On the contrary she accepted it as God's
appointment for her; and, just as some trees when struck with the
ax emit a sweet and delicate fragrance, so the blow of adversity
brought forth faith and beauty in the life of Abigail.

This truth of God's providence she asked David to apply to
his life. He had, indeed, many trials, and was at that time being
hunted for his life by Saul. But Abigail assured him that he
would be delivered out of the hands of his enemies and would
one day come to the throne, for he was "bound in the bundle of
life with the Lord." Since this was so, she pleaded with him not

to sin against God by avenging himself and shedding blood cause-less. She told him it would be no grief unto him and would cause no regret unto him in that day when he had become king that he did not avenge himself, or shed blood causeless. David had indeed many things which we know caused him regret; his great sin against Uriah and Bathsheba; his foolish indulgence of his sons Amnon and Absalom; and, on one or two occasions, his great cruelty as a warrior. But there was one thing that David did not have to regret, and that was due to Abigail's intercession, that on this occasion he did not avenge himself or wipe out the house of Nabal in blood.

What applied to David applies to all of us. He was called to be king. But you and I are "called to be saints," called to be kings and priests unto God! The thought of this is of a nature to keep us back from sin and, because we believe that we are "bound in the bundle of life with the Lord," to teach us to trust ever in his providence.

THINGS WHICH CAUSE REGRET, AND THOSE WHICH WILL NOT CAUSE REGRET

On this occasion David, moved by Abigail's plea and responding to it, and putting aside his wrath and purpose of revenge, broke out into thanksgiving to God for his gracious providence that day. "Blessed be the Lord God of Israel, which sent thee this day to meet me; and blessed be thy advice, and blessed be thou, which hast kept me this day from coming to shed blood, and from avenging myself with mine own hand."

In other words David gave thanks to God for what God had kept him from doing, for what he had not done. There were many things which he had done which he regretted; but he thanked God that he did not need to regret the murder which he had contemplated. Do you ever thank God for the things which you have not done? When we open the book of the past, we come upon some dark and soiled pages which we wish were not there. But as you go through the book of your life, thank God for the record that was not written, for the things, evil things, which God in his grace and providence kept you from doing—as Abimelech, warned in a dream to keep back from great sin against Abraham and Sarah, made offerings of gratitude to God, because God had "withheld him from sinning against God." So let us thank God for the things we did not do.

Then there are the things done which will never cause regret. You will never regret the fact that when you were reviled, you did not revile again; that when you were insulted, you did not answer with another insult. You will never regret that, like Abigail with David, you spoke the "word in season" to another soul. You will never regret that you showed sympathy to the sorrowing, encouraged the despairing, warned the tempted, clothed the naked, or fed the hungry. You will never regret that you remembered your Creator in the days of your youth, or that at an early age you gave your heart to the Lord and came into the church.

At the age of eight years a woman of Harrisburg, Pennsylvania, had united with the church. She told me she had often heard it said that children of that age do not realize what they are doing when they come into the church. But in her case that early commitment to God had been a wall of safety about her when afterward she went to the great city and entered upon her work as a nurse and a social worker. Nothing could be more foolish than to say that a child does not know what he is doing when he comes into the church and pledges his love to the Saviour. I have no doubt that the percentage of those who came at an early age into the church and remained faithful to their vows is higher than that of those who confessed their faith in more mature years. No; none will ever regret that he remembered his Creator in the days of his youth and gave himself to the Lord.

THE BUNDLE OF LIFE AND LIFE TO COME

In this beautiful phrase, "bound in the bundle of life," you can hear too the grand music of immortality. It is one of the clearest notes of the future hope that one hears in the Old Testament. It is not strange, therefore, that this is a verse often inscribed upon the graves of devout Jews. It is indeed true that Jesus "brought life and immortality to light in the gospel." But that does not mean that the hope of it, the expectation of it, was absent from the thought of the Old Testament believer. Immortality is taught in the Old Testament more by inference, assumption, and implication than by direct utterance. Over and over again, and in terms of incomparable beauty, the Old Testament speaks of God's goodness and providence in our life in this world, how we are "bound in the bundle of life." This carries with it the assumption that the soul, for whom God promises so much and does so much by his providence in this life, has a nobler destiny than that of the grave. This double truth, God's providence now in this life and fullness of life in a world to come, is struck over and over again in the Old Testament. This is the note with which the twenty-third psalm comes to a conclusion: "Goodness and mercy shall follow me all the days of my life: and I will dwell in the house of the Lord for ever." As quaint Matthew Henry put it in his comment on that psalm: "All this, and heaven too!" That is, God's goodness and mercy now, and the unknown joys of heaven hereafter. The same note is struck in the seventeenth psalm: "Show me thy marvelous loving kindness. . . . Keep me as the apple of the eye, hide me under the shadow of thy wings. . . . I will behold thy face in righteousness; I shall be satisfied, when I awake, with thy likeness." Likewise the seventy-third psalm: "I am continually with thee: thou hast holden me by my right hand. Thou shalt guide me with thy counsel, and *afterward* receive me to glory." Yes! Because we are "bound in the bundle of life" we look forward to God's great "afterward." God pity the church, God pity the soul, which has no "afterward" in its faith and expectation!

THE WORK OF THE HOLY SPIRIT

This story of Abigail and David is a wonderful setting forth and illustration of the gracious work of God's Holy Spirit. The Spirit speaks through the Scriptures. He speaks in providence: in sickness and in health, in joy and in disappointment. He can speak through hymn and the prayer and the sermon. He can speak, too, through a woman. Here through this gifted woman the Holy Spirit pleaded with David to keep back his hand from sin. David recognized that voice, for he said, "Blessed be God who hath sent you to meet me." God's Holy Spirit has many ways of speaking. No; it is not that he does not speak to us, but that when he does speak, so often we heed him not. The Holy Spirit pleads with us, as he pleaded with David, to know the things which belong to our peace and to refrain from doing that which will cause us future regret and sorrow. And more than that, the Holy Spirit pleads with us to repent of those things which have already caused us regret and sorrow and remorse.

Is there anyone who is marching with drawn sword against God? If so, the Holy Spirit comes to meet you "by the covert of the hill" as he came to meet David. From what does he seek to dissuade you? From an act of revenge? From unfriendliness, hatred, envy, bitter speaking? From disloyalty to the church? From forsaking the Bible and giving up prayer and worship? From hardening your heart? From indulging a sinful desire? Now comes the gracious Pleader, who loves your soul, who knows its high capacity, and who knows the great destiny to which God has called you. Now he comes to plead with you to heed his voice and harden not your heart. Be as wise as David was. Sinner though he was, when he was sure that the Holy Spirit was speaking to his soul, he always obeyed. Therefore he could say, "When thou saidst, Seek ye my face; my heart said, unto thee, Thy face, Lord, will I seek." Obey him! Obey that voice! And you will be "bound in the bundle of life." Then through all the years of this your earthly life, and through all the ages of eternity, it will be no regret to you that when God spoke you answered, and chose Christ and eternal life. Instead of having regret, you will be able to say to the Holy Spirit, as David said to Abigail, "Blessed be God which sent thee this day to meet me."

Other Books for Your Study of Bible Characters

Mark These Men   J. Sidlow Baxter

A treasure house of Bible biographies including Elisha, Elijah, King Saul, Daniel, Gideon, Balaam, and Nehemiah. Also included are New Testament characters such as the Apostle Paul, Lazarus, the rich young ruler, Ananias, and Simon of Cyrene, and many others.

ISBN 0-8254-2197-7   **192 pp.**   **paperback**

The Training of the Twelve   A. B. Bruce

(Forewords by Olan Hendrix and D. Stuart Briscoe.) The monumental classic on discipleship and leadership training. A complete exposition of how Christ prepared His twelve disciples.

ISBN 0-8254-2236-1   **566 pp.**   **paperback**

Great Cloud of Witnesses in Hebrews Eleven   E. W. Bullinger

A classic exposition including an examination of the great heroes of the faith. Full of rich, practical applications.

ISBN 0-8254-2247-7   **462 pp.**   **paperback**

Meet Jeremiah: A Devotional Commentary   Burton L. Goddard

The "Weeping Prophet"— Jeremiah— comes to life in this devotional commentary. With many years of study, teaching and preaching on Jeremiah, Goddard breathes life into this important Old Testament Book.

ISBN 0-8254-2728-2   **160 pp.**   **paperback**

The Apostles of Jesus   J. D. Jones

Dr. Jones' knowledge of human nature, principles of leadership, and how to draw the best out of people, all find expression in his timely study of the Apostles. This treatment deserves to be read carefully, for we have much to learn from "The Twelve."

ISBN 0-8254-2971-4   **192 pp.**   **paperback**

Joshua: Mighty Warrior and Man of Faith   W. Phillip Keller

The author of *A Shepherd Looks at Psalm 23* provides an interesting look at the successor to Moses and conqueror of Canaan. Keller examines the man and mission and gives tranferable and practical insights for those in the "Christian battle."

ISBN 0-8254-2999-4   **184 pp.**   **paperback**

Elijah the Tishbite   F. W. Krummacher

A thorough, analytical work on the character of Elijah. Here is a moving Bible biography that will give the reader new insight into the man, his message, and his ministry.

ISBN 0-8254-3059-3   **208 pp.**   **paperback**

Elisha: A Prophet for Our Time   F. W. Krummacher

A stimulating, fast-paced biography of one of the greatest of the prophets. Dr. Krummacher's warmth and eloquence make compelling reading, while his study of Elisha is thorough and analytical.

ISBN 0-8254-3060-7   **256 pp.**   **paperback**

Great Women of the Bible   Clarence E. Macartney

A collection of sermons from a master pulpiteer of yesterday. Macartney's unique descriptive style brings these women of the Bible to life and provides inspirational reading for all Christians.

ISBN 0-8254-3268-5   **208 pp.**   **paperback**

He Chose Twelve   Clarence E. Macartney

This careful study of the New Testament illuminates the personality and individuality of each of the Twelve Disciples. A carefully crafted series of Bible character sketches including chapters on all the apostles as well as Paul and John the Baptist.

ISBN 0-8254-3270-7   **176 pp.**   **paperback**

Paul the Man   Clarence E. Macartney

Macartney delves deeply into Paul's background and heritage, helping twentieth-century Christians understand what made him the pivotal figure of New Testament history. Paul, the missionary and theologian, are carefully traced in this insightful work.

ISBN 0-8254-3269-3   **208 pp.**   **paperback**

Women of the Bible   Frances Vander Velde

Character studies of over 30 women with lively discussion questions included. Excellent for women's Bible study groups.

ISBN 0-8254-3951-5   **260 pp.**   **paperback**

Available from your Christian bookstore, or

kregel
PUBLICATIONS

P.O. Box 2607, Grand Rapids, MI 49501